legal rights to child-friendly working hours:

a practical guide to using sex discrimination law
by Camilla Palmer

This edition published in Great Britain 1998
by the Maternity Alliance, 45 Beech Street,
London EC2P 2LX.

© Maternity Alliance 1998

British Library Cataloguing in Publications
Data A CIP catalogue record for this book
is available from the British library

Design by Synergy EC1
Typesetting by Boldface EC1
Printed by WBC Book Manufacturers Ltd

ISBN
0 946741 50 6

The law is stated as at November 1998

Acknowledgements
This book, the accompanying leaflet, the database of advisers and supporting training
courses could not have been produced without generous funding from the Nuffield
Foundation.

Caroline Underhill (Bristol Law Centre), Kate Wood (EOC) and Hilary Plews (Waltham
Forest CAB) made most helpful comments on the text and we are grateful to everyone
at the EOC, Bristol Law Centre and the Maternity Alliance for trialling the book.

Christine Gowdridge, Joanna Wade, Chris Smith, Sophie Robinson, Elaine
Seth-Smith, Bridget Orr, Linda Stavrianakis, Sue Felgate of the Maternity Alliance have
all given invaluable help in a great variety of ways.

Equal Opportunities Review kindly gave permission to reproduce their article on the
EC childcare good-practice guide. (EOR 77 January February 1998)

Maternity Alliance is funded by London Boroughs Grants.

The Maternity Alliance is a national charity working to end the inequality and promote the well-being of all pregnant women, new parents and their babies. Amongst its aims are an improvement in the working lives of parents so that they are better able to balance work and family life and a challenge to unfair and unequal treatment at work of pregnant women, mothers and other primary carers.

The Maternity Alliance runs training courses and provides publications on most aspects of maternity rights and benefits including a leaflet "Child-friendly working hours: your legal rights" (£1.50). Its advice line, which runs a national database of advisers who can take on sex discrimination cases, is open both to employees and employers on 0171 588 8582. Maternity Alliance, 45 Beech Street London EC2P 2LX.

Camilla Palmer is a consultant solicitor with Bindman and Partners working exclusively in the field of discrimination and maternity rights. She teaches and writes extensively and has written Maternity Rights and Discrimination at Work published by the Legal Action Group.

legal rights to child-friendly working hours:

a practical guide to using sex discrimination law by Camilla Palmer

Related law:

Procedure and enforcement:

Appendices:

Key points

Diagnosing indirect sex discrimination

Chapter 3: Is there a requirement or condition?   27

Chapter 4: Is there a disproportionate adverse impact on women?   33

Women who **can** comply cannot complain of indirect sex discrimination 51

The woman must have suffered a disadvantage as a result of the child-unfriendly hours 52

She must show that: 53
▶ she has been forced to resign; or
▶ she has suffered some other disadvantage, eg being forced to work long hours which results in excessive demands on time and energy and consequent stress; or
▶ she has been forced into a lower paid job in order to work part-time

Chapter 6: Has the employer justified the requirement or condition? 55

The employer must show: 55
▶ objective justification on grounds other than sex for the working hours required; and
▶ the hours correspond to a real need by the employer; and
▶ the hours are appropriate to meet the need; and
▶ the hours are necessary to meet the need

Examples of justification put forward by employers: 61
▶ we have a policy of not allowing part-time work
▶ it is not possible at managerial level
▶ full-timers are more efficient
▶ there will be duplication of work
▶ it is more expensive
▶ we need continuity
▶ it will set an undesirable precedent
▶ we have reached saturation point
▶ long hours are necessary for leadership and motivation of junior staff
▶ The employee is not reliable

There should be equal access to training for part-time workers

It will usually be unlawful discrimination to select part-timers
before full-timers for redundancy

Chapter 8: The case for child-friendly working hours

A woman must first think about what hours she wants and
how these will fit in with the job, eg
► what is the top and bottom line
► why can't she work full-time
► how can the particular job be done on different hours
► employer's likely response and how to negotiate

What to request? Consider:
► part-time working
► job-sharing
► flexible hours
► working school hours and/or term
► working from home
► shift swopping
and be prepared to negotiate different options if possible, and
offer solutions to perceived problems

Remember the business case, ie that child friendly working
hours for jobs at all levels leads to:
► increased efficiency, enthusiasm, morale and commitment
► the competitive edge for the employer
► being able to attract and retain high calibre staff
► the likely increase in maternity leave returners
► decreased sickness absence and other absenteeism
► reduced recruitment and training costs (for new staff)

- ▶ returning to work on the same hours as before;
- ▶ accepting less favourable terms or self-employment in order to work part-time;
- ▶ resign, but consider first:
  - – the financial implications
  - – the problems in getting another job
  - – whether there is any scope for further negotiation

Chapter 11: Relevant provisions of the Sex Discrimination Act 1975   113

- ▶ job applicants,
- ▶ employees,
- ▶ the self-employed,
- ▶ partners,
- ▶ contract workers

Discriminatory acts which are prohibited are:
- ► offering a woman less favourable terms and conditions;
- ► not employing a woman because she is a woman
- ► not giving a woman the same opportunities for transfer, training or promotion
- ► giving a woman fewer or less favourable benefits, facilities or services
- ► dismissing a woman (including constructive dismissal)
- ► subjecting a woman to a detriment

Refusal to allow a woman to work child-friendly hours may 119
entitle a woman to resign and claim both under the
Employment Rights Act and the SDA;
Compensation for direct and indirect sex discrimination

Chapter 12: Relevant European law 121

UK law must be interpreted in line with EC law, and in 121
some cases it may override conflicting UK law

Relevant provisions are:
- ► Article 119 of the Treaty of Rome which provides for equal pay (including benefits connected with work);
- ► Equal Treatment Directive which has similar provisions to the SDA
- ► The European Council Recommendation on Childcare and the Guidance
- ► The Working Time Regulations which lay down minimum health and safety requirements relating to working hours

Chapter 13: Maternity Rights 127

All women, irrespective of length of service, pay, hours of 127
work, are entitled to 14 weeks **basic maternity leave**; during

this period the contract continues

Women who have worked for the same employer for two years (at the 11th week before the EWC) are entitled to return to work up to 29 weeks after the beginning of the week the baby was born; this is **extended maternity absence**; it is unclear whether the contract continues

129

Entitlement to maternity leave and absence is dependent on the woman giving the appropriate notices

128

Some women have more favourable contractual rights which can be claimed over and above the statutory rights

130

All women have a right to return to the **same** job at the end of the 14 weeks maternity leave

131

Women entitled to extended maternity absence are entitled to return to the same or failing that to an equivalent job; a demotion (even on the same pay) is not an 'equivalent' job

132

Chapter 14: Unfair and constructive dismissal — 135

Failure to allow a woman to return to work is a dismissal; the dismissal may be:
▶ unfair dismissal under the ERA, and/or
▶ discriminatory under the SDA

135

A dismissal may occur where there is a contract of employment and
▶ the employer dismisses the employee
▶ a fixed term contract expires without being renewed
▶ the woman is not allowed to return to work after maternity absence
▶ the woman resigns in response to the employer's breach of contract (this is **constructive dismissal**)

The dismissal may be fair (if on one of the specified grounds) or unfair if either:

137

- ▶ there is no 'fair' reason (unfair dismissal) or
- ▶ it is connected with the woman's pregnancy, childbirth maternity leave or absence (automatically unfair dismissal)

Chapter 15: Procedure for bringing a case

Chapter 16: Remedies and compensation

Chapter 17: Legal advice and funding a claim

The Equal Opportunities Commission can provide help and assistance, by way of advice, help with drafting letters and legal documents, advice leaflets — 177

A trade union member should always seek help from the union

Although there is no full legal aid, applicants on a low income can get advice through the 'green form' scheme — 178

Applicants with insurance policies should check the policy to see if they have legal expenses insurance

Some solicitors and barristers will do work on a contingency fee (no win no fee) basis — 179

Chapter 1

The context

'How can it be discrimination for an employer to refuse to allow a woman to work part-time?' asked a Court of Appeal Judge recently in a sex discrimination case.[1]

Many people, lawyers and senior judges included, understand very little about using the sex discrimination law to argue for women's right to work child-friendly hours. The aim of this book is to enable women to negotiate and, where that fails, to enforce, through the Sex Discrimination Act 1975 (SDA), child-friendly working hours.

Women as carers and paid workers

One of the main changes in the labour market over the past 20 years has been the increasing number of women combining work with childcare. No longer is the traditional family unit based on a man in full-time work and a woman in a domestic role. Women now combine childcare with paid employment, often involving long hours. In 1996 67% of women returned to work within 11 months of having a baby compared with 45% in 1988.[2] Long, inflexible or irregular hours are incompatible with primary responsibility for children, particularly babies.

The demand for 'child-friendly' working hours

Many women returning from maternity leave want to adjust or reduce their hours to enable them to combine work and family. The most recent survey found that about one-third of women returning from maternity leave changed from full-time to part-time work on their return. One quarter of women who did not return said this was because they could not find a job with the right hours.[3] Although some women are forced or even choose to return to lower paid, lower status jobs in order to be able to reduce their hours, women should be able to return to the same job on the same terms and conditions – but with child-friendly hours.

There are also women who do return full-time but find that the pressures of work and family are intolerable and so they seek to reduce their hours after a period of full-time working.

The right to return to the same job is under the Employment Rights Act 1996 (ERA) (see chapter 13). Although there is no 'right' to child-friendly working hours, a refusal to allow them may be discriminatory under the SDA, not the ERA.

Fathers

A man may be able to argue for reduced or different hours if a woman in the same situation would be allowed them; to refuse a change in hours would be directly discriminatory against the man (see p26).

Advantages to employers of child-friendly hours

There are many advantages for employers in allowing women to work hours which suit their childcare needs, including greater motivation and productivity, lower staff turnover, continuity during sickness and holidays and improved morale (see chapter 8).

Child-unfriendly hours: flexibility for employers

Flexible working is also used by employers to improve their competitive edge, for example, to meet fluctuating demand for labour and 24 hour service delivery.[4] The trend towards 24 hour services and the move from permanent full-time employment to insecure short term contracts and agency work means that workers, fearing for their jobs, feel pushed into working longer hours. Research has highlighted the degree to which employees feel compelled to work excessive hours in a climate of insecure employment.[5] An inability or refusal to accept this long hours culture is seen as a 'lack of commitment' to the job, irrespective of whether the long hours make the worker any more productive or efficient or the effect on the employee's health.

Overtime and anti-social hours requirements are usually child-unfriendly working hours and arrangements. These may also be challenged as discriminatory (see p27).

The needs of employers and employees

The needs of different employers and employees are enormously varied. Employers have a range of needs. Some hospitals, supermarkets and banks, for example, need 24 hour cover, others, like tourism, have to deal with seasonal peaks and troughs.

Employees also need a range of options. While many women can only work office hours (9am to 5pm) because childcare is only available then, others want to work outside these hours when their partner or another member of the family is not working and can care for the children. Some women can work full-time but not do hours of overtime. Others want to work part-time, particularly if they are lone parents or their partner works long hours. Some women cannot afford to work part-time. Others cannot work full-time because they cannot afford paid childcare and rely on family and friends who are not available full-time. Women with school age children are more restricted by school holidays; women with young babies are not.

There are innumerable permutations of needs and wishes determined by factors such as childcare, age and number of children, family income, partner's working hours, location and requirements of the job.

The future: Fairness at Work

On of the three main elements of the framework for the future in the White Paper on Fairness at Work,[6] is to implement 'policies that enhance family life while making it easier for people – both men and women – to go to work with less conflict between their responsibilities at home and at work.' It is recognised that helping employees to combine work and family life satisfactorily is 'good not only for parents and children but also for businesses' and that many successful modern companies, both large and small, have adopted a culture and practices in support of the family. These include flexibility over hours and working from home to allow parents to spend more time with their children.

With the increasing number of part-time workers, it should be possible for employers to accommodate employees wanting to work different hours. What is crucial is that flexible working is accepted as a positive advantage by and to both employee and employer. Only then will there be the necessary commitment for it to work in practice. As Prime Minister, Tony Blair, said in his Foreword: 'My ambition for this White Paper goes far wider than the legal changes we propose. It is nothing less than to change the culture of relations in and at work – and to reflect a new relationship between work and family life'.

There are currently no Government proposals to make child-friendly hours available to working parents as a right.

The Maternity Alliance

The Maternity Alliance provides information on the law as it now stands. However, its ultimate objective is to press for improvement and clarification to the law to give all parents, not just women, a clear right to work child-friendly hours unless their employers can show the job cannot be done on such hours. This is the only way of enabling all women and men to reconcile their work and family commitments. In the meantime, all the arguments available are set out in this book. They are complex and often obscure, but they are the best that exist.

Footnotes

[1] *Cast v Croydon College* [1998] IRLR 318 CA, where a woman was arguing it was indirect sex discrimination for the employer to refuse to allow her to return part-time.
[2] *Maternity Rights and Benefits in Britain 1996*, Social Security Research Report No 67, Callender C, Millward N, Lissenburgh S, and Forth J, Policy Studies Institute (1997).
[3] See footnote 2.
[4] *Flexibility Abused*, NACAB (1997).
[5] *Go Home on Time Day*, Parents at Work (1996).
[6] *Fairness at Work*, Department of Trade and Industry, Cm 3968 (1998).

Chapter 2

Overview of the law

The law is important as a negotiating tool – 'a carrot'. If negotiations fail it can turn into a 'stick' to force an employer to offer child-friendly hours or to compensate a woman denied a job or forced to leave one.

1 What are child-friendly hours?

Child-friendly hours, also known as family-friendly hours, non-standard working, equitable flexible working, part-time and flexible working, are working arrangements which enable women (and men) to combine paid work with childcare. Child-unfriendly hours are the opposite.
Child-friendly hours include:
▶ part-time working and job-sharing
▶ flexible hours to suit childcare arrangements
▶ term time working
▶ working from home for part of the time
▶ career breaks and sabbaticals
▶ fixed hours not subject to change by the employer at short notice.

2 How can the law be used?

The law is a useful tool for negotiation and also a means of forcing the employer to allow child-friendly arrangements. This book is intended to clarify the legal rights of working parents, provide guidance on negotiating child-friendly hours and advice on how to take a legal case.

Remember
Negotiate first, following the advice in Chapter 8 and do not necessarily accept what you are told, especially when it is different from the advice in this book.

3 When can the law be used?

a After maternity leave

A woman returning from maternity leave has the right to return to the **same** or equivalent job on the same terms and conditions. If she wants to return on child-friendly hours, a woman should not be forced into a job which is inferior either in pay, status, or security (see p131ff). If a woman follows the route described in this book in order to get child-friendly hours, she should not have to accept down-grading or inferior terms and conditions.

b If full-time hours become impossible

A woman may be able to argue for child-friendly hours if she finds it impossible to cope with her existing working arrangements (see p96).

c When applying for a new job

Job applicants are also protected by the Sex Discrimination Act (see Chapter 11).

d If the employer changes the hours

Where an employer insists on changing the woman's hours to child-unfriendly hours, this may be indirect sex discrimination and breach of contract.

e On adoption

The same principles should apply to women who have adopted children, whether or not they are taking time off. It is still usually the woman who has main responsibility for the children and so cannot work child-unfriendly hours.

4 Why indirect discrimination?

A refusal to allow a woman to work child-friendly hours will often be an example of indirect sex discrimination but it will not always be immediately obvious why. It is helpful to look at why the concept of indirect discrimination was introduced. The Sex Discrimination Bill originally prohibited only direct discrimination, the less favourable treatment of a person on the grounds of her/his sex. However, the lesson from the United States was that there were more subtle forms of discrimination which had the **effect**, if not **the intention**, of excluding women from the labour market. Thus, it was important to prohibit unjustified practices which **operated** in a discriminatory way. This is indirect discrimination and the SDA prohibits it.

Account must be taken of the particular circumstances of the job-seeker or employee. Men can generally work full-time, not usually being constrained by the needs of their children. Women with children are less likely to be able to work full-time. Only if jobs are available part-time or on a job-share or on flexible hours will there be equal access to jobs for men and women.

Thus, in order to enable women generally to compete equally with men in the labour market, the law prohibits certain employment practices which place women at a disadvantage compared to men. However, this does not apply where the practice is necessary for the particular job.

5 How to diagnose indirect sex discrimination: the four key questions

a   Is there a requirement or condition to work child-unfriendly hours?

In order to establish indirect discrimination a woman has to show that her employer has imposed some form of requirement or condition. To do this first consider the **opposite** of child-friendly working arrangements, for example, full-time working, inflexible hours, overtime, changing shift patterns. These are all 'requirements' which are more likely to disadvantage women. For example, for a woman who wants to work part-time but is refused, the 'requirement' is to work full-time.

A woman usually needs to have asked for and been refused the hours she wants before it is clear exactly what the condition or requirement is.

b   Is there a disproportionate adverse impact on women?

It is necessary to show that a requirement, such as full-time working, is one which has a disadvantageous impact on women compared to men. The woman must be able to show that a considerably smaller proportion of women than of men can comply with the requirement. That is, there is a 'disparate impact'. Statistical evidence must be produced to support this. This can be done in two ways (preferably both):

▶ by looking at the impact in the particular workplace;
▶ by looking at national statistics; for example, 80% of part-time workers are women.

c   Has the woman suffered a disadvantage because she cannot comply?

There are many reasons why full-time working is incompatible with caring for babies and children. These include the difficulty of finding good quality, affordable childcare which fits in with working hours, the stress which often results from working long hours and looking after young children, the relationship between the parent and child, any special needs of the baby or child, and the need to breastfeed for a longer period than maternity leave allows.

d   Has the employer justified the requirement or condition?

All the other elements of indirect discrimination may be established but there will be no discrimination if the employer can show that the hours imposed are necessary for the job. The woman should highlight all the well-documented advantages of child-friendly working arrangements (see p87ff). She should also be able to deal with all the reasons put forward by the employer to justify the hours required.

The four key questions to ask when diagnosing indirect sex discrimination are summarised in the table on the next page.

How to diagnose indirect sex discrimination: the four key questions

	Questions asked in the Sex Discrimination Act	What they mean	Examples	How to answer the question	Is there a case for unlawful sex discrimination?
1.	Is there a requirement or condition applied to male and female employees by their employer?	Is there a practice in the workplace that disadvantages women because of their childcare responsibilities?	This could be: ▶ full-time work ▶ long working hours ▶ overtime requirements or ▶ irregular shift patterns	Identify the requirement or condition	If the answer to question 1 is yes, go on to question 2
2.	Is there a disproportionate adverse impact on women?	Does the practice have a worse impact on working women than it does on men?	Labour market statistics show that many women cannot work full-time. 80% of part timers are women and this is primarily because they are caring for children or adult dependants.	Identify the pool for comparison and do the proportions test. The pool is generally employees doing similar work in that workplace with account being taken of the wider workforce.	If the answer to question 2 is yes, go on to question 3.
3.	Has the woman suffered a disadvantage because she cannot comply with the requirement?	Can the woman show that she is personally disadvantaged by the practice (e.g. the requirement to work full-time) because she cannot comply with it ?	An individual's childcare responsibilities may make it impossible for her to work full time so that she has to resign from her job.	A woman must show that she cannot in practice work full-time. A preference for part-time is not enough.	If the answer to question 3 is yes, go on to question 4.
4.	Has the employer justified the requirement or condition?	Can the employer show that the working hours required are necessary for the job to be done effectively?	It would be hard for the Prime Minister to job-share because absolute continuity is needed although many senior posts are now job-shared.	The employer cannot say a blanket 'no'. S/he must provide objective justification for a refusal ie good business reasons.	If the answer to question 4 is no, indirect discrimination has been proved.

6 Definition of indirect sex discrimination in the Sex Discrimination Act 1975

Under the Sex Discrimination Act (SDA) a person discriminates against another if:

> he applies to her a requirement or condition which he applies or would apply equally to a man but –
>
> (i) which is such that the proportion of women who can comply with it is considerably smaller than the proportion of men who can comply with it; and
>
> (ii) which he cannot show to be justifiable irrespective of the sex of the person to whom it is applied; and
>
> (iii) which is to her detriment because she cannot comply with it.

The same provisions apply to indirect discrimination against married women.[1]

7 Need to show a 'prohibited act'

The woman must also show that the employer has done something which is prohibited under the SDA, ie

▶ has put her under a disadvantage (by being forced to work child-unfriendly hours, or being forced to resign) and/or

▶ has dismissed her (including constructive dismissal).[2]

8 Equal Opportunities Commission Code of Practice

Tribunals must take account of the Equal Opportunities Commission Code of Practice: For the elimination of discrimination on the grounds of sex and marriage and the promotion of equality of opportunity in employment (1985) which provides that:

> 'There are other forms of action which could assist both employer and employee by helping to provide continuity of employment to working parents, many of whom will have valuable experience or skills.
>
> Employers may wish to consider with their employees whether certain jobs can be carried out on a part-time or flexi-time basis.'

Failure to take account of the Code, for example, by not considering whether jobs can be done part-time or on a flexi-time basis may lead to a finding of discrimination. The failure is not in itself unlawful but it may be taken into account by a tribunal or court.[3] In *Berry* and *Hinks*,[4] the EAT held that tribunals were required to have regard to any breach of a code of practice. Account should also be taken of the European Community (EC) Recommendation on Childcare.[5] (See Appendix 2.)

9 European Community law

Relevant European provisions and their implications for discrimination law in the UK are set out in Chapter 12.

Remember
Tribunal procedures can be used to get information from the employer. Throughout the following chapters on how to prove indirect discrimination, relevant procedures are highlighted. The detail is in Chapter 15. The most important procedures are:

▶ the **questionnaire**;
▶ **request for further and better particulars of the ET3**;
▶ **discovery**; this is a means of obtaining all relevant documents from the employer;
▶ **written answers**; this can be a useful way of obtaining answers to specific questions.

10 Marital discrimination

A married woman should always argue indirect marital discrimination as well as indirect sex discrimination.[6]

The Sex Discrimination Act outlaws discrimination against married women compared to single women. It may be indirect marital discrimination to deny married women child-friendly working hours. Married women are more likely to have children than single women. This may be useful if there are only women in the workplace or if the statistics in the workplace are unhelpful for proving indirect sex discrimination.

The same arguments could be used for married men but in practice it is unlikely that the statistics can show that they have more childcare responsibilities than single men.

11 Men refused child-friendly working hours

Men cannot claim indirect sex discrimination in the same way as women; in general the adverse impact of child-unfriendly hours is on women not men. However, where a woman is allowed to work child-friendly hours, a refusal to allow a man in a parallel situation, for example, doing similar work and having childcare responsibilities, to work such hours may be direct discrimination.

Note
Less favourable treatment of part-time workers (than full-timers) is likely to be unlawful indirect discrimination (see Chapter 7).

Note
Employment tribunal decisions are not binding on other tribunals. They are useful examples of how the law may be interpreted in any one case.

Footnotes

[1] SDA sl (1) (b) and s3. See Appendix 1.
[2] SDA s6(2)(b). Dismissal includes constructive dismissal SDA s82(1A).
[3] SDA s56A(10).
[4] *Berry v Bethlem and Maudsley NHS Trust and Hinks v (1) Riva Systems and (2) Lumsden* (1997) 31 DCLD.
[5] *Council Recommendation on Childcare 92/24/EEC and Work and Childcare: implementing the Council Recommendation on Childcare – a guide to good practice,* Social Europe, Supplement 5, (1996).
[6] SDA s3 and see *Hurley v Mustoe* [1981] IRLR 208; [1981] ICR 490.

Chapter 3

Is there a requirement or condition?

Before identifying the practice which disadvantages her, it is important for the woman to consider what hours she can and cannot do and the extent to which she is willing and able to be flexible (see p85). Relevant factors are:

► childcare (availability, quality, affordability);
► the presence (or absence) of the father or other carer;
► particular problems of the children (e.g. medical or behavioural);
► the stress of long hours (including travel);
► how the job could be done on different hours (including potential problems and how to deal with them).

1 Examples of requirements

The following are examples of requirements:
► to work full-time;
► to work overtime;
► to work until 6pm or later;
► to work antisocial hours;
► to be office-based all week;
► to do early or late shifts;
► to spend nights away;
► to change hours at short notice;
► to enter into a new contract to work new rostering arrangements.

It is important for an applicant to work out and define the requirement or condition.

There may be more than one requirement or condition.

Remember

A requirement or condition may be explicit, for example, full-time worker required, or implied, for example, the job is office-based. It does not have to be in writing.

2 'Requirement' and 'condition' should be interpreted very widely

In *Holmes*,[1] the appeal case which established that refusing to allow a woman to work part-time may be indirect discrimination, the Employment Appeal Tribunal (EAT) said that the words 'requirement' and 'condition' should be interpreted broadly and could include a requirement to work full-time.

3 Legal confusion about meaning of 'requirement' and 'condition'

Some employers try and avoid liability by adopting a very legalistic approach to the technical definition of indirect discrimination. They are not usually successful. One argument is that 'full-time working' is not a 'requirement', since this would require a person to 'do a certain act' or 'it is just part of the job'. This argument was used in *Clymo*[2] but it must be wrong and is not usually followed (see *Clarke* and *Holmes* below).

Case examples

In *Clarke*,[3] where part-timers were to be made redundant before full-timers, the employer argued that a procedure whereby part-time workers were dismissed first could not be a requirement, as a requirement meant that the person had to 'do a certain act'. The EAT disagreed, saying that a requirement or condition meant a provision which a person has to fulfil to obtain a benefit, such as working full-time. The EAT said that:

> *'The purpose of the draughtsmen in using both words must have been to extend the ambit of what is covered so as to include anything which fairly falls within the ordinary meaning of either word and should not be given a narrow construction.'*

So, the requirement was 'that in order not to be made redundant it is a requirement that you work full-time'.

In *Holmes*,[4] where a woman argued for the right to work part-time after maternity leave, the EAT said:

> *'Requirement or condition are plain words of wide import fully capable (for example) of including an obligation of full-time work and there is no basis for giving them a restrictive interpretation in the light of the policy underlying the Act or in the light of public policy.'*

Similarly, the Northern Ireland Court of Appeal (NICA) in *Briggs*,[5] held that the fact that the nature of the job requires full-time attendance does not prevent there being a 'requirement' (see also *Gordon* below).

How to deal with wrong law: *Clymo*

If wrong decisions are raised by employers, it is important to show why they are wrong. In *Clymo*,[6] the EAT said that the employers had not applied a requirement of full-time working. Full-time working was a requirement of the terms of employment but was not something which the employers had positively 'applied' to the woman. It was part of the job.

In *Clymo* a dubious distinction was made between different types of jobs; if a cleaner had to work full-time, this would be a 'requirement', whereas for a managing director it would be in the nature of the appointment and not a 'requirement' or 'condition'. This interpretation is clearly wrong and has not been followed by any appeal court.[7] In *Gordon*,[8] the EAT said that they preferred, 'without hesitation', the Holmes approach, not *Clymo*. They recognised that:

> *'as a matter of policy, that in relation to sex discrimination the widest possible definition should be given to the Statute to embrace, at least in principle, the widest possible classes of case'.*

The EAT further said that *Clymo* was isolated and 'correctly so'.

Clymo is inconsistent with European Court of Justice (ECJ) decisions and the definition of discrimination in the *Draft Directive on Burden of Proof* (see p125).[9] For example, the ECJ have held in *Bilka*,[10] that a practice which in fact affects more women than men infringes Article 119 of the EC Treaty unless the employer can prove that the measure is objectively justified. (see p55)

4 More than one requirement or condition?

There may well be more than one requirement or condition. It is quite common, for example, for a woman to ask to job-share and to be refused. She may then ask if she can do a four day week. If she is again refused, she may ask if she can work from home on one day. If this proposal is rejected, she may ask if she can work through her lunch hour in order to get home earlier. If the job involves substantial overtime, the woman's final position may be that she will return full-time but cannot do the overtime. In these circumstances, the employer may have applied up to four different requirements,

► to work full-time, and/or
► to work fixed, inflexible hours from 9am to 5.30pm, and/or
► to work from the office every day, and/or
► to do (substantial) overtime.

If this happens, the requirements can all be argued as alternatives.

Note

Although it is not necessary to specify the requirement(s) in the Notice of Application to a Tribunal IT1), the complaint must be clear and it is important to identify it at an early stage because:

a   the employer may ask for further details of the requirement (in a request for further and better particulars); and

b   it will be necessary to show that each requirement has a disproportionate impact on women; and

c   the woman will need to show that she cannot comply with the requirement; and

d   it is always helpful to ask the employer for details of how they can justify each requirement. It is important that the requirements are argued not only in the alternative but cumulatively (as above).

More wrong law: is the requirement an absolute bar?

In some race discrimination cases the courts have held that where a requirement or condition is only a 'preference' or simply one of many factors taken into account, there is no 'requirement'.[11] This has long been considered wrong and the EAT, in a sex discrimination case, *Falkirk*,[12] confirms this. The EAT held that a liberal interpretation should be given to the words 'requirement or condition'. If it is shown that qualifying for a benefit (in this case a requirement for management training and supervisory experience) is more difficult for women than men in the workplace, this is a condition or requirement.

5 When was the requirement or condition applied to the applicant?

The question is whether the woman **could comply** with the requirement or condition at the time it was applied to her. It is not relevant that she **could** have complied with it at a different time or may be able to in the future. The requirement is applied by the employers when they refuse to allow a woman to change her hours.

It will not be a requirement or condition unless it has been imposed. The possibility of a requirement being applied in the future is not enough, for example, where a woman is told she may have to change her hours in the future.

6 The request for changed hours must have been refused

There is no requirement or condition unless the employer has refused a request for child-friendly working hours. In *Graham*,[13] the tribunal found that the employer had said the job-sharing application would be given fuller consideration. It had therefore not been refused at the time the applicant resigned, even though the employer was 'discouraging'. However, the tribunal added that, if nothing was done actively to further the application, 'there must come a point at which the employee is entitled to consider that whatever the employer is saying, in practice he is putting so many obstacles in the way of the application that they are tantamount to a refusal' (see p108ff).

7 Time limits

The time at which the requirement is applied may be important because of the time limits within which a claim must be brought. There is a danger that if a woman asks to work child-friendly working hours **before** going on maternity leave and is refused, the three month time limit for bringing proceedings will run from this refusal (see p144ff).

8 Remember: use the questionnaire

The questionnaire (see Chapter 15) is helpful for identifying the requirement. The employer can be asked what working hours are required and when and where they are required to be worked, as well as how this is justified. If there is no reply to the questionnaire, similar questions can be asked by way of written questions (see p151).

Footnotes

1   *Home Office v Holmes* [1984] IRLR 299.
2   *Clymo v Wandsworth LBC* [1989] IRLR 241.
3   *Clarke v Eley Kynock Ltd* [1982] IRLR 482.
4   see footnote 1.
5   *Briggs v North Eastern Education and Library Board* [1990] IRLR 181 CA.
6   see footnote 2.
7   See *Briggs*, footnote 5, which, although a NICA decision and not binding, is persuasive.
8   *United Distillers v Gordon* EAT/12/97 unreported 23 May 1997.
9   *Draft Directive on Burden of Proof* 97/C 302/02, EOR 76 Nov/Dec 1997.
10 *Bilka-Kaufhaus GmbH v Weber von Hartz* [1986] IRLR 317. See also *Enderby v Frenchay Health Authority and Secretary of State for Health* [1993] IRLR 591 and also footnote 12.
11 *Perera v Civil Service Commission* (No.2) [1983] IRLR 166 and *Meer v London Borough of Tower Hamlets* [1988] IRLR 399.
12 *Falkirk Council and others v Whyte and others* [1997] IRLR 560 and EOR 75 Sept/Oct 1997.
13 *Graham v City of Glasgow DC* Case No. S/550/89 Glasgow 24.7.89.

Chapter 4

Is there a disproportionate adverse impact on women?

Some tribunals will take a 'common knowledge' view that women are less likely to be able to work child-unfriendly hours than men (see p40). However, unless the employer concedes that there is an adverse impact on women, it is not safe to rely on the tribunal adopting this approach. In *Mawkin*,[1] or example, the tribunal said there was only statistically insignificant evidence about the particular hairdressing salon where there were five women and one man. All were single but one woman had a child. No attempt was made by the applicant to show what the situation was generally in relation to a requirement to work evenings/shifts. The case was lost because the tribunal wanted statistics that were not available.

Where possible, women should be ready to show statistically, both in the workplace and the labour market, that a particular requirement or condition hurts women more than men or married women more than single women.

Note that, although there are similarities between the use of 'common knowledge' to show, on the one hand, that fewer women in the work-force can comply with a requirement and, on the other, that the particular woman **cannot** comply with the requirement (see Chapter 5), the former is an objective test based on the effect of a practice on women generally and the latter is concerned with the effect on the applicant. Common knowledge is likely to be more significant in proving the adverse impact on women generally.

1 Choosing the comparators: who do you need to compare?

Indirect discrimination involves imposing requirements which, while they appear to be neutral between men and women, ie they are applied equally to men and women, have a greater adverse effect on women. To show this is happening two groups must be compared – 'the comparators' – to show that one is suffering a worse impact. The comparison may be between male and female employees in the workforce or men and women in the labour market generally. The same comparison applies to married women and unmarried women. A tribunal can infer adverse impact from labour force statistics, especially if statistics are not available on the particular workforce.

The question to be asked in each case is what is the group of men and women to be compared? This is the relevant pool.

Where an existing employee is challenging child-unfriendly working hours, the pool is generally the workplace or the employees in it to whom those hours are applied by the employer.

Thus, where the comparison is limited to the workforce, the pool is men and women doing similar work. It is generally not appropriate to compare a secretary with a managing director; they are not doing similar work.

In *Edwards*,[2] the Court of Appeal held that the pool was the section of the relevant workforce which is affected or potentially affected by the requirement. In this case it was all train drivers to whom the new rostering arrangements were to be applied.

However, some tribunals are content to rely on common knowledge sometimes supported by labour force statistics. In *Convery*,[3] the tribunal dealt with the issue of the pool briefly and broadly, saying:

> *'We are entitled, as an industrial jury, to rely on our experience and common sense to determine that the proportion of women who can comply with a requirement to be full time teachers is smaller than the proportion of men.'*

Example

A female administrative officer in a large company with five departments wants to return to work part-time. The requirement is 'to work full-time'. Is the comparison between:

a female and male administrative officers in her department,
b female and male administrative officers in the company,
c all men and women in the company.
d the labour force.

The correct answer is probably either (a) or (b), but taking into account (d). These groups are doing similar work. Remember that in discrimination claims like should be compared with like. It is best to get figures for both. However, if there are only women and no men in groups (a) and (b), it is not possible to compare the women with men. It is then necessary to look at the whole company (c) and/or the labour force.

Marital discrimination

The comparison may also be between married and unmarried women in those groups to show marital discrimination. This is particularly important where there are no men in the group – in which case the only comparison is between married and unmarried women. However, this will only apply if the applicant is married.

Possible pools for sex or marital discrimination

Sex discrimination	Marital discrimination
Women and men in the same grade in the same department	Married and unmarried women in the same grade in the same department
Women and men in the same grade in the workplace	Married and unmarried women in the same grade in the workplace
Women and men in the same department	Married and unmarried women in the same department
Women and men in the labour force	Married and unmarried women in the labour force
Women and men in the labour force doing the same job	Married and unmarried women in the labour force doing the same job

Note
In each group it is necessary to find out:
▶ the number of male and female part-timers and full-timers
▶ the number of married and unmarried female part-timers and full-timers.

Remember

The questionnaire and written question procedure can be used to get information about the breakdown of full and part time employees in the workplace. (see p143)

2 Who decides the pool?

It is for the tribunal to decide on the pool and it is difficult to challenge their decision. There is a danger that the pool which the tribunal considers appropriate is one which has not been considered by the parties and there are therefore no statistics before the tribunal. It is therefore useful for the parties to try and agree the pool before the hearing or to work out the statistics for all possible pools. But beware, the tribunal could still decide to have a different pool.

3 How to calculate the 'proportions'

The test under the SDA is whether the **proportion** (not number) of women who can comply with a requirement is considerably smaller than the **proportion** of men who can.4 This is calculated by:

a   taking the number of women in the relevant pool (say there are 60 female administrative assistants in the workforce); and

b   taking the number of women in the pool who can comply with the requirement, in this case to work full-time (say there are 45 full-time female administrative assistants); and

c   dividing (b) by (a); this gives the proportion of women in the pool who can satisfy the requirement, 75%; and

d   taking the number of men in the pool (say there are 100 male administrative officers in the workforce); and

e   taking the number of men in the pool who can comply with the requirement, in this case to work full-time (say there are 95); and

f   dividing (e) by (d); this gives the proportion of men in the pool who can satisfy the requirement, 95%.

The proportions are then compared. This is referred to as the 'proportions test'. Is 75 % considerably smaller than 95 %? If it is, disproportionate impact has been proved.

	a Total no of staff	b Full-time staff	c Part-time staff	% of staff who can comply	% of staff who cannot comply
Female	60	45	15	75% $\frac{45 \times 100}{60}$	25% $\frac{15 \times 100}{60}$
Male	100	95	5	95% $\frac{95 \times 100}{100}$	5% $\frac{5 \times 100}{100}$
Total	160	140	20	20 percentage points difference	

What 'considerably smaller' means is discussed in section 7 below.

4 Problems with workplace and/or labour force information

a The most relevant statistics may not be available, for example, the number of male and female, married and unmarried, full-timers and part-timers in the workforce. Information about other types of child-unfriendly hours is even less likely to be available. There are few figures on homeworking, working overtime, fixed hours. It will then be necessary to rely on labour force statistics or 'common knowledge' (see below).[5]

b The statistics may be distorted, possibly by discrimination. For example, if an employer has a policy against employing part-timers, there will be no male or female part-timers so it will not be easy to show disproportionate impact. There may also be historical reasons why there is a small number of women (or men) in the workplace (see p38).

c The disproportionate impact in the workplace may be very small. In a small workplace, this may be because of a change in staff, for example, one part-time woman has left and one part-time man has replaced her. The applicant may be the only worker who cannot work full-time (see p41).

d   There may be fortuitous circumstances affecting the numbers within the pool or within either group, or affecting the ability of particular group members to comply with a condition which is not typical of the usual position.

In *Edwards*,[6] the CA accepted that these last three circumstances applied and should be taken into account when deciding whether five per cent was a considerably smaller proportion. (see p41) The proportions test in this case had shown that 100% of the 2,023 male operators in London Underground could comply, compared with 95.2%, 20 out of 21 women, a difference of just under five per cent.

If the only person wanting part-time work or other child-friendly hours is the applicant and there are no other part-timers in the workforce, it is very difficult to establish that there is a disproportionate impact on women; the only person affected is the applicant and there is no one with whom to compare her. This was, however, sufficient in *Edwards*.

The reason that there are no part-time workers may be because the employer does not allow employees to work part-time and this itself may be discrimination. In *Schaffter*,[7] the High Court said that there must be no discrimination in the selection of the pool and this is particularly important where the figures have been distorted because of discrimination.

The option, if there are no part-timers, is for the pool to be widened to include everyone in the department (not just administrative assistants) or the whole workforce, or to rely on general statistics about men and women in the labour force. In some cases, the tribunal will accept labour force statistics as proof of disparate impact without the need to produce detailed evidence from the particular workforce.

Labour force statistics are likely to be a more accurate reflection of the patterns of employment of men and women, married and single women than workforce information. They also show that, even though there may only be a small percentage difference, it is usually not fortuitous but is linked to women's primary responsibility for childcare.

5 Labour force statistics

The tribunal can infer from labour force statistics that, for example, a greater proportion of women than men work part-time and this is because they are more likely to have childcare responsibilities.

Labour force statistics shows the pattern of women's and men's employment. They show, for example, that the majority of part-timers are women, that the rise in part-time work has coincided with women's increased employment and that women work part-time because of child-care responsibilities. This is important in order to prove that women work part-time in order to combine paid work with childcare.

Relevant labour force information will include:

▶ statistics and research showing the proportion of women in employ-ment who have primary responsibility for a child, in contrast with the proportion of men in that position;
▶ statistics showing the relative number of men and women working full-time, doing overtime, and other types of working arrangements;
▶ statistics showing why women and men work part-time.

Similar statistics should be obtained in relation to married and unmarried women to show marital discrimination. A summary of existing statistical material and important sources of information are set out in Appendix 1 and analysed in the table below:

Men and women in the labour force who can comply with a requirement to work full-time

	All men and women in the labour force	Men and women with children aged 0-4	Men and women with children aged 5+
% of men who can comply	92.5	96.9	97.4
% of women who can comply	57.1	36.0	41.4
% difference between the number of men and the number of women who can comply	**35.4**	**60.9**	**56.0**

Source: *Labour Force Survey* 1997

6 The importance of 'common knowledge'

Tribunals will often take account of their 'common knowledge' that women take primary responsibility for children and for this reason want shorter and more flexible hours to fit in with their childcare arrangements. In *Stimpson*,[8] the tribunal said it would use its 'common sense' to find that the proportion of women who could comply with a requirement to work full-time is considerably smaller than the number of men.

In *Edwards*,[9] the Court of Appeal upheld the EAT decision that the tribunal was entitled to have regard

> *'to its common knowledge about the proportionately larger number of women than men in employment with primary childcare responsibilities'.*

In *Briggs*,[10] the NICA also said that a tribunal can take into account its own knowledge and experience when deciding whether a requirement has a disproportionate impact and elaborate statistical evidence was not always necessary. The Court of Appeal made similar comments in *Meade-Hill*,[11] which concerned a requirement to work in any part of the UK. This had a disproportionate impact on women who, as secondary earners, would find it more difficult to comply than men.

Remember

It is important to obtain and present evidence about:
► the workplace figures,
► labour force statistics and common knowledge
in relation to the working hours and arrangements of male and female workers, married and unmarried female workers.

7 What is considerably smaller?

There is no rule as to what amounts to 'considerably smaller'. The courts have refused to adopt any figure, or range of figures, as to whether one proportion is considerably smaller than another.[12] However, this does not mean that there has to be a large difference. With a large pool one or two percentage points can represent a large number of people. It is for each tribunal to decide what is considerable. Relevant factors include:

a   the extent of the difference between the proportion of women and proportion of men who can work full-time or other child-unfriendly hours; it is worth looking not only at the proportion of women who cannot comply, compared to men who cannot comply, but also the proportion of women who can comply compared to the proportion of men who can comply;

b   the length of time there has been a difference in proportions; if there has been a persistent difference between the proportions of women and men who can work full-time, this will be significant because it shows a consistent pattern. Both consistency and persistency are apparent from the labour force figures which show that over the past 20 years over 80% of part-time workers have been women (see Appendix 3);

c   where using the proportions test the difference is insignificant, tribunals should also take into account **numbers** of male and female part-time workers as the European Court has done.

Case examples

In **Edwards**,[13] the applicant, a female single parent, was a train driver. Her rostering arrangements allowed her to be at home in the mornings and evenings to look after her son. In 1991 the employers announced a new flexible shift system under which her duties were to begin at 4.45 am and were to include Sundays. Her complaint of indirect sex discrimination was upheld by the tribunal.

The tribunal found that all the 2,023 male train drivers could comply with the new rostering arrangements and Mrs Edwards was the only one of 21 female train drivers who complained that she could not comply with the new arrangements. The arrangements only adversely affected one woman. The proportion of women who could comply with the new arrangements was 95.2% (20 out of 21) compared to 100% of men. The employer appealed to the CA on the basis that 95.2% was not considerably smaller than 100% and there was no adverse impact.

The CA upheld the tribunal finding that 95.2% was 'considerably smaller' than 100%.

The CA in *Edwards* made the following important points:

▶ there must be a substantial and not merely marginal discriminatory effect (disparate impact) as between men and women;

▶ the disparate impact should be inherent in the application of the requirement and not simply a result of unreliable statistics or fortuitous circumstances; thus, it must not be 'coincidental' that the requirement hurts women disproportionately;

▶ there is flexibility in relation to the question of whether a particular percentage is 'substantially smaller' in any given case;

▶ a tribunal does not sit in blinkers and the members are selected in order to have a degree of knowledge and expertise in the industrial field generally. The high preponderance of single mothers having care of a child is a matter of common knowledge;

▶ the tribunal was entitled to have regard to the large discrepancy in numbers between male and female train drivers. This showed that it was either difficult or unattractive for women to work as train drivers;

▶ it would be wrong to ignore entirely the striking fact that not a single man was disadvantaged by the requirement despite the vast preponderance of men within the group.

The combination of a small difference in the workplace figures together with the labour market statistics and 'common knowledge' was enough. The applicant was successful.

In *Seymour Smith*,[14] the CA said that too much emphasis should not be given to the need for the difference to be 'considerable'. It pointed out that European law provides that

'there shall be no discrimination whatsoever on grounds of sex'.

In *Seymour Smith* a difference of 7% was sufficient; 67% of women could comply with the requirement, in this case the two-year threshold for unfair dismissal claims, compared to 74.5% of men. Sixty-seven point four percent is 90% of 74.5%. In this case the court was impressed by the 'consistency' and 'persistency' of the figures over a long period.

8 What happens if the woman is applying for a new job?

If a woman wants to apply for a new job with the same or a different employer on a part-time basis, she can still argue that a requirement to work full-time is discriminatory (see p77). The comparison in such a case may be between the male and female job applicants. However, this may distort the position as few women wanting to work part-time will apply for a full-time job. The pool may more appropriately be men and women in the geographical area from which job applicants may come. However, the problem with this is that the information is unlikely to be available on a regional basis. The most appropriate comparison would therefore be between men and women in the labour force, or, if the information is available, qualified men and women in the labour force. Statistics on qualified men and women are generally very hard to find. The EOC may have some limited information available.

Footnotes

1. *Mawkin v The Cats Whiskers* Case No. 07494/9ILS/B London South 13.8.91.
2. *London Underground v Edwards* (No 2) [1998] IRLR 364, CA; it is being appealed to the HL.
3. *Convery v The Governers Rawthorpe Infant and Nursery School* (1) *Kirklees Metropolitan Council* (2) Case No. 1800057/1998 Leeds IT.
4. Note, however that the difference in numbers may be relevant as the European cases rely on proportions and/or numbers.
5. 'Common knowledge' is often referred to as 'judicial notice'. See for example, *Cassidy v British Telecommunications and Manpower plc* Case No. 2500061/96 and 2500063/96 Carlisle IT 22.1.97 and *Cheal and Walker v Sussex Alcohol Advice Service* Case No. 34889/94 and 36691/94 Brighton IT 23.2.95.
6. See footnote 2.
7. *R v Secretary of State for Education ex p Schaffter* [1987] IRLR 53, HC.
8. *Stimpson v Dewjoc Partnership* Case No. 61562/94 Middlesborough IT 15.5.95.
9. See footnote 2.
10. *Briggs v North Eastern Education & Library Board* [1990] IRLR 181, CA.
11. *Meade-Hill and NUCPS v British Council* [1995] IRLR 478.
12. See footnote 2.
13. See footnote 2.
14. *R v Secretary of State for Employment, ex p Seymouth Smith* [1997] IRLR 464, CA and [1997] IRLR 315 HL. This case has been referred to the ECJ by the House of Lords.

Chapter 5

Has the woman suffered a disadvantage because she cannot comply?

There are few appeal decisions on what is required to show that a woman 'cannot comply with a requirement or condition'. It is increasingly being argued that women **can** comply with a requirement to work full-time because they can buy childcare.

Although some tribunals rely on 'common knowledge' that a woman cannot work full-time because of her childcare responsibilities, it is not safe to rely on this.

1 Choosing to work part-time is not enough

The woman must be able to show that she **cannot in practice** comply with the requirement or condition, for example, to work full-time. A preference for part-time work is not enough. She should consider all the reasons why she cannot work full-time (see p48ff).

Many women need to work part-time (or other child-friendly hours) in order to look after their children. They do not have to show that it is **'impossible'** to work the required hours but that it would not be practicable (see below).

Case examples

In **Price**,[1] the EAT said that a woman:

> *'is not obliged to marry, or to have children, or to mind children; she may find somebody to look after them and as a last resort she may put them into care. However to say that for those reasons she can comply with a requirement to work full-time would be wholly out of sympathy with the spirit and intent of the Act... it is relevant in determining whether women can comply with the condition to take into account the current usual behaviour of women in this*

respect as observed in practice, putting aside behaviour and responses which are unusual.'

In *Gulson*,[2] the employer argued that the applicant could comply with a requirement to work full-time because she could employ a full-time nanny, whether living in or living out. The employer's representative wanted to ask Mrs Gulson detailed questions about the family outgoings in order to show that by spending less the couple could afford a full-time nanny. The tribunal refused to allow the representative to go into a detailed financial analysis similar to that used on division of assets in divorce proceedings. The tribunal pointed out that the question of whether Mrs Gulson could comply with the changed hours was not limited to the question of whether or not she could afford a nanny. There were many other points for consideration which were relevant to the issues between the parties. This was upheld by the EAT who held that:

> *'The tribunal had identified that this financial question was only one of many considerations that was relevant for its consideration'.*

In *Gordon*,[3] the EAT held that:

> *'The decision to insist on full-time working discriminates against any woman with childcaring responsibilities who applies for the job. Equally, although nursery facilities can be made available, we do not consider that precludes the view that a mother with childcaring responsibilities meets the non-compliance test'.*

The EAT said that, although each case would have to be looked at carefully to look at the practical implications of compliance, there could be 'little doubt that a mother with a very young baby is at least capable of meeting the test' (of not being able to comply with a requirement to work full-time).

Wrong law: *Clymo* again

In *Clymo*,[4] the EAT upheld the tribunal decision that the applicant could work full-time. The tribunal said:

> *'At this level of income, and most particularly in the London area, with child-minding facilities readily available, people of these qualifications and this combined income and with a professional career both behind*

and ahead of them could certainly conduct their family arrangements on less old-fashioned bases than the less qualified and more lowly paid'.

In *Clymo* the employer had offered childcare, it was necessary for only three days a week, the family income was sufficient to pay for childcare and the tribunal said that her desire to care for her child was a personal preference. This decision is inconsistent with *Holmes*,[5] *Price*,[6] *Briggs*,[7] and *Gordon*[8] and has not been followed by any appeal court and very few tribunals.

The fact that there is childcare available does not *necessarily* mean that the woman can comply, but she must show reasons why she **cannot** comply. It is a matter of fact and she should produce evidence to support this.

Case examples

The fact that a woman has main responsibility for children does not necessarily mean that she will be able to show she cannot work full-time. In *Dinmore*,[9] the tribunal found that it was only the woman's 'choice and wish not to work full-time' and this was not sufficient. Yet in other cases, tribunals have accepted that the woman had valid reasons for 'not wishing to work full-time'.[10]

In *Snook*,[11] the woman had told her employer she could return full-time because her baby would be cared for by relatives who lived nearby. She then changed her mind. The tribunal found she **could** work full-time because:

▶ she initially said she could work full-time, as both sets of parents lived near her;
▶ she only wanted to work part-time for two or three months;
▶ she was prepared to leave her child for whole days at a time;
▶ as she intended to leave him full-time after a further three months, there was no practical reason why she could not have made that decision earlier.

In *Snook*, the tribunal said that if the claim had been for unfair dismissal they would have found for the woman because the employer 'singularly failed to discuss with the applicant ways in which she could carry out her duties in a flexible manner operating from her home for some of the week to enable her to look after her child and offering flexibility for a temporary period'. If the applicant had instead argued there was a requirement to work inflexible hours for a temporary period and there were good reasons for this, such as continuing to breastfeed, she may have succeeded.

Note

Women should be careful not to say that they can work full-time or other child-unfriendly hours. It is important to gather as much evidence as possible to show why it is not possible to work the hours required.

2 Why do women need child-friendly hours?

A woman needs to consider why she cannot work the required hours and produce evidence to support this. Common reasons are:

a Lack of available and affordable childcare

Some women **cannot** work the hours required either because there is no childcare available or because it is too expensive. In many cases, women rely on parents, relatives or friends for cheap or free childcare and they may only be available on certain days or during specific hours. For example, in *Stimpson*,[12] the tribunal found that the applicant had made a reasoned legitimate decision that she could not work full-time, having regard to the prohibitive cost of childcare for two children, but could manage part-time with assistance from her parents. Having properly made her decision, the tribunal accepted she could not comply with a requirement to work full-time and it was to her detriment.

A requirement to work overtime at short notice is particularly difficult because it is often impossible to find childcare, especially if the overtime is early in the morning or late in the evening.

b The stress of combining long hours at work and childcare

Some women can afford childcare but do not feel able to cope with the stress of working long hours. Working full-time and/or long hours is undoubtedly very stressful, particularly if the woman is a lone parent or has a partner who works long hours. In *Burston*,[13] the tribunal said that the applicant found the full-time job 'very demanding and exhausting and she was not able to carry on with that permanently'. It continued by saying

> 'We think that is sufficient to show, in practical terms, that she cannot comply with it. It is not necessary to show that it was physically or absolutely impossible for her to have worked full-time and it is not necessary to show that there were no possible ways in which she could have carried on working five days a week, for example, by persuading her husband to take over childcare responsibilities or by obtaining further domestic help to cut down her obligations in the evenings'.

Similarly, in *Todd*,[14] the tribunal acknowledged the enormous stress for the woman leaving her child at a childminder for all his waking hours. She could not therefore comply with a requirement to work full-time.

c   Tasks which cannot be delegated to a carer

It may be that childcare could, in theory, be delegated to a carer. However, some women feel that being absent from home for up to, say, ten or eleven of the twelve hours a baby is awake is not in their or the baby's interests. The pressure is even greater when a baby or child is ill. In addition, there are tasks which cannot easily be delegated. These include:

► being able to continue breastfeeding during the morning and evening (see below);
► visits to the doctor or health clinic, particularly where there is concern about the baby's welfare;
► visits to the nursery to discuss a baby or child's progress;
► maintaining links with the child's school and, in particular, class teacher, and attending school events, such as assemblies or sports days;
► dealing with any emotional problems the baby or child might have;
► hospital visits, particularly if the baby or child may need an operation which could involve a stay in hospital.

d   Other pressures

There are other factors which may be relevant including:
► the number of other children;
► the hours worked by the woman's partner and his involvement in childcare;

▶ whether the woman is a lone parent.

The long hours culture clearly takes its toll on all workers but particularly parents with young children. In many cases, the birth of the second child makes full-time working even more difficult.

In *Barrett*,[15] the tribunal accepted the applicant's evidence that the stress of both her and her husband working full-time, coupled with the pressures at home led to her feeling very run down and ill. In addition it was a strain on the marriage. The tribunal found that the requirement that she work full-time meant, realistically, that she could not work at all. For the advantages of shorter working hours to employers see p87ff.

In *Todd*,[16] the tribunal also acknowledged that children are often more demanding as they get older.

e   Breastfeeding

A woman may want to work part-time in order to continue breastfeeding. The employer may be prepared to agree to her working part-time temporarily before returning full-time. That will generally depend on what arrangements can be made to fill the other part of the post.

General health and safety requirements

If there is a risk to a breastfeeding worker or the health or safety of her baby, the employer must take reasonable measures to ensure that, by temporarily adjusting the working conditions and/or the working hours of the employee concerned, the exposure of that employee to such risks is avoided.[17] If it is not possible to alter the woman's working conditions or hours of work, the employer must consider offering her suitable alternative work where this is available.[18] If there is no suitable work, the woman is entitled to be suspended on full pay. The details of these provisions are outside the scope of this book.[19]

If it can be shown that a requirement to work long hours is a risk to the health of either the mother or baby, or that breastfeeding is necessary for the health of the baby and cannot be done with the woman working such hours, the employer should take reasonable steps to reduce or vary her hours or, if this is not possible, take the steps outlined in the paragraph above.

A woman can, in addition, claim indirect sex discrimination under the SDA. In *Squillaci*,[20] the woman was advised by her GP and the National Eczema Society that she should breastfeed for one year. She asked if she could return to work part-time for a period of six months, during which time she could continue breastfeeding by expressing one feed. The tribunal found that the woman was prepared to be flexible and work part-time on a temporary basis but the employer had rejected this out of hand without any consideration as to how she could achieve her objective. It was therefore indirect sex discrimination.

3 Common knowledge

Some tribunals adopt a common sense view and accept that a woman cannot work full-time. For example, in *Todd*,[21] the tribunal said 'women do leave employment because they cannot manage well both jobs of being mother and worker. What usually happens...is that women take their maternity leave, return to work for about three months and leave for good. It is not an unusual pattern; it occurs in industry and commerce as well.'

4 Women who can comply

There are women, however, who could easily work full-time or overtime but would prefer shorter hours. This may be because they have no children or their partner is not working and can care for the children. For example, in *Tomlinson*,[22] the woman's husband had just been made redundant and was looking after the child three days a week. This meant that the woman could work full-time. Such women will not be able to show that they **cannot** comply with the requirement. It is their choice to work part-time and that is not sufficient to prove indirect discrimination. However, if their partner needs time to look for another job and/or finds a job, it is then arguable that he is no longer available for childcare and so the woman cannot then comply with a requirement to work full-time.

Note

The same principles apply to marital discrimination. Married women are less likely to be able to work child-unfriendly hours than unmarried women because, at present, a greater percentage of married women have children than unmarried women.

5 Effect of full-time return

If a woman returns full-time because she cannot afford to be without work, the employer may argue that she **can** work full-time as she is doing so. In *Todd*, the applicant asked to use her leave entitlement in order to enable her to work part-time during the first few months after returning to work. There is a danger the employer will then argue that she is unreliable or abusing the system even though it is a contractual right. A tribunal should not be sympathetic to such a response, particularly if no objection has been made to this use of the holiday. It is important, however, for the woman to get the employer's agreement to take holiday in this way.

6 Has the woman suffered a disadvantage?

As we have seen, a woman cannot complain of indirect sex discrimination unless she cannot comply with the requirement, in this case to work child-unfriendly hours, at the time it was imposed. In addition, she must also show she has suffered a detriment (see p24).

A detriment – or disadvantage – may be:

a   being forced to resign because she cannot work the hours required; this may also be constructive dismissal (see p138);

b   being forced to work the required hours which, in *Holmes*, the EAT said was resulting in 'excessive demands on her time and energy' (see also *Todd*);

c   being forced into a lower paid job in order to work part-time.

All a woman should have to show is that she has personally suffered some disadvantage.

More wrong law: *Clymo*

In *Clymo*, the EAT did not accept that a requirement to work full-time was to the woman's disadvantage because she could not comply with it. The EAT said:

'in trying to fit society into the framework of the statute and the statute into our society, in every employment ladder there will come a stage at which a woman who has family responsibilities must make a choice'.

This is an extraordinary comment. The purpose of the indirect sex discrimination provisions is to enable women to combine work with childcare; quite the opposite of the EAT's view in *Clymo*. This is an isolated decision and is inconsistent with *Holmes, Price, Gulson, Briggs* and European law (see p46).

Footnotes

1   *Price v Civil Service Commission* (No 2) [1978] IRLR 3.
2   *Zurich Insurance Co v Gulson* Case No. EAT/747/97.
3   *United Distillers v Gordon* Case No. 12/97 23.5.97, EAT unreported
4   *Clymo v Wandsworth LBC* [1989] IRLR 241.
5   *Home Office v Homes* [1984] IRLR 299.
6   See footnote 1.
7   *Briggs v North Eastern Education and Library Board* [1990] IRLR 181, CA.
8   See footnote 3.
9   *Dinmore v 1 Dorset County Council 2 Governors of Martin Kemp Welch School* Case No. 49345/94 Folio No. 3115/61.
10 *Watt v Ballantyne and Copeland* S/1262/94 Glasgow IT 22.8.84.
11 *Snook v A C Electrical Wholesale plc* Case No. 36218/96.
12 *Stimpson v Dewjoc Partnership* Case No. 61562/94 Middlesborough IT 27.2.95.
13 *Burston v Superior Creative Services Ltd* Case No. 72892/95.
14 *Todd v Rushcliffe Borough Council* Case No. 11339/90 Nottingham IT 1.2.91.
15 *Barrett v Newport Borough Council* Case No. 34096/91 1.7.92.
16 See footnote 14.
17 Management of Health and Safety at Work Regulations reg 13A(2) and *Pregnant Workers Directive*, 92/85/EEC Article 5.
18 ERA ss 66,67.
19 See *Maternity Rights*, Palmer C, LAG (1996).
20 *Squillaci v W S Atkins (Services) Ltd* Case No. 68108/94 London South 21.1.97.
21 See footnote 14.
22 *Tomlinson v Transport Hospital Fund* Case No. 26173/93.

Chapter 6

Has the employer justified the requirement or condition?

The test of justifiability is often the most important issue in indirect discrimination claims. Even if the woman proves everything else, she will lose if the employer can show that the working hours or arrangements required are necessary for the job. The tribunal will look at the employer's reasons for wanting the job done full-time. The woman should think carefully about the job, what is involved, how it has been done in the past, what happens when she goes on holiday or is sick and whether the employer has made any effort to accommodate her request.

It is of crucial importance to gather as much evidence as possible to show that a job can be done part-time or on other child-friendly hours or that overtime is not necessary. Although the burden is on the employer to show justification, the woman should be prepared to rebut the reasons put forward by the employer. It is important to find out what arguments the employer will rely on by using the questionnaire procedure (see p143). Sections 7-9 of Chapter 8 set out the advantages to employers of child-friendly working hours.

1 Legal principles

a   The test

The main test for justification was laid down in a European case, *Bilka*,[1] in which a part-time worker challenged the exclusion of part-timers from the employer's occupational pension scheme. The ECJ held that a practice which has a disproportionate adverse impact on women is justified if

▶   it can be objectively justified on grounds other than sex,
▶   it corresponds to a real need on the part of the employer,

- ▶ is appropriate with a view to meeting that need, and
- ▶ is necessary to meet that need.

This is the *Bilka* test. It is generally considered to be the most useful explanation of justification under the SDA.

Although the ECJ will normally leave the national court to decide what is 'justified', in an important decision, *Hill*,[2] the Court did provide guidance about what would not constitute justification, ie 'general assertions unsupported by objective criteria' (see p58) and 'increased costs' (see pp64 and 78).

Remember

The Burden of Proof Directive, which has not yet been implemented, states that the practice must be appropriate and necessary and able to be justified by objective factors unrelated to sex (see p125).

b The link between the discriminatory effect and justification

The greater the impact of the practice in relation to:
- ▶ the number of employees affected, and/or
- ▶ the seriousness of the impact on any individual,

the harder it will be for the employer to justify.

In *Edwards*,[3] the EAT said that

> '...although there is no direct correlation between the two we would anticipate that in accordance with the purpose of the Equal Treatment Directive (ETD) of eliminating discrimination between the sexes in the employment field, the less justification London Underground had for the way they treated Ms Edwards, the less likely it is that a tribunal will conclude that she has failed to show that the disproportionate effect of the condition was considerable'.

In *Jones*,[4] the CA held that tribunals should therefore look at the practice to assess:
- ▶ how many women will or are likely to suffer because of the requirement or condition, and
- ▶ how much damage or disappointment the practice may cause to employees and how lasting or final is the damage.

Case example

In *Hampson*,[5] the Court of Appeal said that it is necessary to strike a balance between the discriminatory effect of the requirement or condition and the reasonable need of the person who applies it. It is not sufficient for the employer merely to establish that it considered its reasons to be adequate.

Thus, the tribunal can take into account the particular hardship suffered by the woman, bearing in mind the extent to which these hardships apply to other employees. If the imposition of, say, a requirement to work full-time means that a woman has no alternative but to resign and give up work, this is a serious consequence and the onus on the employer to justify the requirement should be greater.

c   The justification itself must not be discriminatory

The employer must show that the requirement is justified, apart from the sex of the worker. In other words, the reason why the requirement is justified must not itself be discriminatory.

Case example

The EOC challenged statutory provisions which excluded part-time workers from certain employment rights such as protection from unfair dismissal and redundancy pay. The EOC argued that the provisions were indirectly discriminatory because of the adverse impact on women, who form the majority of part-time workers.

The Government argued that the aim of the longer qualification periods was to increase the availability of part-time work. This, they said, would be achieved by reducing the costs to employers of employing part-time workers.

The House of Lords accepted that an increase in part-time work was a beneficial social policy aim but pointed out that the same result would follow from paying part-time workers a lower basic rate than full-time workers. This would be a 'gross breach of the principle of equal pay' and could not possibly be regarded as a suitable means of achieving an increase in part-time employment. The justification itself would have had a discriminatory effect.[6]

d Generalised statements by the employer are not enough

Although some tribunals do accept generalised statements by the employer, such as 'there were good commercial reasons', the employer should be pressed to substantiate them. In *Gordon*,[7] the EAT said that it is 'not sufficient that the employer believed his reasons behind the decision in question to be justified'. Justification must be 'objectively established'. An employer may argue, for example, that part-timers

▶ are not so integrated in the workforce, or
▶ do not have the same commitment, or
▶ are more expensive to employ, or
▶ 'do not fit in', or
▶ no other employer allows part-time working.

These reasons should be supported by evidence. For example, how are part-timers more expensive and by how much; what is the evidence that they are less integrated in the workforce and less committed?

Case example

In the EOC case,[8] the Government argued that the aim of the longer qualification provisions was to increase the availability of part-time work by keeping the cost of employing part-timers down. The House of Lords did not accept that the provisions (requiring a minimum number of hours work per week) had actually resulted in greater availability of part-time work as the Secretary of State produced no evidence to support this. Such a generalised claim, unsupported by the evidence, did not constitute justification.

In *Rinner-Kuhn*,[9] the German Government argued that the exclusion of part-time workers from a sick pay scheme was justified because part-time workers (working less than ten hours per week) were not integrated into the undertaking in the same way as full-time workers. The ECJ said that this was a generalised statement and so was not regarded as 'objective criteria unrelated to any discrimination on grounds of sex'.

In another German case, *Nimz*,[10] part-timers were required to have longer years of service than full-timers before being promoted. The ECJ held that, in order to justify such a practice, the employer must show that there is a relationship between the length of service and the improved performance. Although, seniority often goes hand in hand with experience, and should in principle enable an employee to carry out her tasks better, the employer should provide evidence of this.

Sometimes tribunals accept the employer's word that a requirement for full-time work, fixed hours, or overtime, for example, is necessary, without investigating whether this is really the case. The appeal courts, including the ECJ, have required employers to provide concrete evidence as to how they justify a practice. In *Seymour Smith*,[11] the CA held that 'We have found nothing in the evidence, either factual or opinion, which obliges or enables us to draw the inference that the increase in the threshold period has lead to an increase in employment opportunities'. The same principles should apply in tribunals.

Is there a harsher test for the State?

Some cases indicate that it may be more difficult for the State to justify a discriminatory legislative policy than individual employers. However, there is no logical reason why this should be the case and the decisions involving legislative provisions are binding on tribunals. However, it is often easier for the State to justify indirect sex discrimination in social security rather than employment matters because the courts have allowed the State considerable discretion to determine matters of social security.

e A question of fact and law

Ultimately, the question of whether a requirement or condition is justifiable is primarily one of fact. The facts must be interpreted according to the *Bilka* test. Each case will have to be considered on its merits and will depend mainly on the type of job and whether it can be done with different working hours or arrangements.

Relevant factors may include:

► the size of the employer; the larger the employer, the easier it should be to accommodate part-time workers;
► the type of job; clearly a receptionist cannot work from home;
► whether the job has previously been done successfully on a part-time or job-share basis.

a   One way of countering the employer's reasons will be to show the 'business need' for child-unfriendly hours can be satisfied in another way

Women wanting child-friendly working arrangements should point out to their employers different options by which they can meet the needs of the business in a way which is not discriminatory (see Chapter 8). For example:

▶   a full-time job could be job-shared;

▶   a demand for long hours could be satisfied by employing another person;

▶   employees could be given a choice about whether they work late or early shifts;

▶   flexi-time could be introduced to enable employees to have some choice about their working hours.

Remember

New Ways to Work, an organisation promoting flexible working arrangements, have publications that give general information on alternative forms of child-friendly hours.(see Appendix 2).

b   Using other employers as good examples

Employers will put forward different reasons for insisting on full-time working, overtime etc, depending on the type of job and their perception of how the work should be organised. These reasons may be challenged by employees by showing that other employers allow child-friendly working in similar jobs (see below). New Ways to Work will have information on employers who provide child-friendly working arrangements, but they will charge for this.

Try and find examples of similar types of jobs which have been successfully done part-time or with child-friendly working arrangements.

In *Barrett*,[12] the applicant pointed out that a neighbouring borough, Cardiff, had introduced job-sharing and, in a letter to the EOC, had described the benefits:

'Without exception all those managers questioned had found the initiative to be an invaluable human resource tool which resolved many recruitment and selection difficulties and which in most instances led to higher levels of productivity. The initial anxieties expressed before the operation of this initiative such as it being difficult to manage or leading to staff conflict were not borne out in any instance'.

The applicant also pointed out that many other local authorities advertised jobs as being open to job-sharing. The tribunal found that the Council's blanket policy against flexible working was unlawful discrimination.

Note
If the employer subsequently allows other workers doing similar work to job-share or work part-time, that will be strong evidence that the job can be done part-time. It will be hard then for the employer to justify the previous refusal.

3 Common justifications

a There is a blanket policy against job-sharing/part-time work

Some employers say they have a policy not to allow part-time work or job-sharing. This cannot be objectively justified where the employer has given no consideration to whether the job can be done on different hours. A blanket policy where no account is taken of individual circumstances is likely to lead to a finding that the employer has not justified the requirement.

There may be a policy in relation to a particular job. In *Stimpson*,[13] the employer argued that the fact that the job had always previously been full-time in some way justified the refusal to consider part-time employees. The tribunal said this was 'not a good reason at all. The very purpose of the legislation is to protect against discrimination and to avoid previous practices which may have proved to have been discriminatory' (see also p58).

Remember

Find out if there is a policy, whether written or simply practice. It may be apparent from, for example:

▶ a document, which could be a policy document, a letter or memo stating that part-time work is not allowed, minutes of a meeting;

▶ previous practice, particularly if other employees have asked whether they can work part-time and have been refused;

▶ conversations in which the employer has said s/he does not like part-time work;

▶ the employer's previous response to requests to work part-time or job-share.

The questionnaire or written answer procedure can be used to ask whether the employer has a policy on part-time work or job-sharing.

Case examples

In *Barrett*,[14] management refused to consider an application from a housing assistant to job-share because they were committed to a policy of full-time working. The tribunal found this to be discriminatory.

In *Hicks*,[15] the tribunal found that the Council's refusal to allow the applicant to job-share or work part-time was due to an objection which was 'a matter of principle against part-time teachers, nothing less and nothing more' as they had used part-timers freely in the past for cover for absent teachers. The refusal therefore was not objectively justified.

In *Watt*,[16] the tribunal held that the refusal to allow a job-sharer to return to work on a job- share basis was discriminatory. The tribunal found the employer merely felt it would be more convenient to recruit a full-time employee and this was not enough to show justification.

b Job-sharing is not possible at supervisory or managerial level

Some employers consider that a job which involves managing or supervising staff cannot be done on a part-time or job-share basis. However, evidence from New Ways to Work shows that managerial jobs can be job-shared. For example, jobs such as personnel director, police sergeant, solicitor, principal social worker, senior lecturer, research manager and business development analyst have all been job-shared.[17]

One justification put forward is that it would be difficult for job-sharers to manage full-time employees and, in particular, there is a need for consistency in discretionary decisions by managers. There is also the danger of employees playing one job-share manager off against the other. One solution to this is for each job-share to manage different people and cover for each other only when it is unavoidable. It is, as always, important to show how the management responsibilities could be shared effectively.

The onus is also on the job-sharers to show that they can ensure consistency of decision- making and effective communication (see p99). This may involve each job-sharer being available to discuss urgent matters with the other job-sharer when she is not normally working.

It is important for senior management to support the job-share arrangement and unreasonable failure to do so may be less favourable treatment and therefore discrimination.

Case example

In *Given*,[18] Mrs Given, who managed 10 to 12 team members was told when she asked to job-share that it was a policy that at her grade there could be no job-sharers. The employers justified this on the basis of 'operational' matters and referred to the need for continuity given the importance of handling customer complaints. There was no proper assessment of the applicant's duties and difficulties which might be encountered in job-sharing. The tribunal was not satisfied that there were any meaningful operational difficulties and upheld the complaint of discrimination. Mrs Given was awarded compensation of £35,000 made up of £3,000 for past loss of earnings, £27,000 for future loss of earnings and £5,000 for injury to feelings (see p167).

c   Full-timers are more efficient

In *Quarterly*,[19] the tribunal said there was no evidence that two part-time workers would not be as efficient as one full-time worker.

d   There would be duplication of work

In *Squillaci*,[20] the employer said that time would be wasted in job-sharers liaising and reporting to each other and this would be an inefficient use of resources. The tribunal was impressed by the applicant's meticulous record-keeping and felt that the employer had not discussed how she would ensure the work was done satisfactorily (see p64). Assumptions were made without basis. For example, many job-sharers communicate important matters in their own time.

e   There are extra costs

Some employers say that allowing part-time work or job-sharing is too expensive. There may be extra costs in management time if two employees need to be managed, as opposed to one. However, the degree of management required and time involved will be crucial. The employer should be made to justify an assertion that it is more expensive. The employee may be able to show that it may be **less** expensive overall, because of savings in recruitment and training costs if she is forced to leave and has to be replaced (see Chapter 8).

Case examples

In *Holmes*,[21] the Home Office argued that their costs would increase if they took on two part-time workers instead of one full-time worker. The EAT preferred the applicant's evidence that the Civil Service was losing valuable trained personnel when they left to start families and in some departments efficiency increased when part-timers were introduced.

f   Continuity would be impossible

Employers often argue that a full-time worker is needed for reasons of continuity. However, as the tribunal pointed out in *Cheal*,[22] the problem of lack of continuity is often more imagined than real. In *Stimpson*,[23] the tribunal held that a refusal to allow a receptionist to work part-time was not justified. The employer's need for continuity could be met, said the tribunal, by the simple means of a notepad to record messages and outstanding calls.

Case examples

In *Barrett*,[24] the employers argued that a housing assistant's job could not be job-shared because of the need for contiuity. The tribunal found that although continuity was an advantage in all jobs, it did not make job-sharing undesirable nor impracticable. In particular, they pointed out that cover had to be arranged during annual leave, sickness and maternity leave. If an employee was out of the office, another employee could pick up a file and deal with an enquiry; there were also others who were familiar with the work.

In *Squillaci*,[25] the applicant, a draughtswoman, kept detailed records of each job including day-to-day matters which were important to the job. Site visits were recorded with details of discussions and material events. The tribunal commented that the applicant was 'meticulous in the way she maintained records'. Site meetings were scheduled in advance. Urgent incidents rarely occurred. The applicant could not think of any circumstances that might arise with which only she could deal.

In *Clay*,[26] a teacher of English asked if she could job-share on her return from maternity leave. The school refused saying that it was not in the educational interests of children for there to be job-sharing. The head teacher said that job-sharing created a lack of continuity and had a disturbing effect upon the education of the children.

The tribunal found it to be significant that the County Council (Leicestershire) had a job-sharing scheme for school teachers. It therefore said that informed opinion in the education field must be that job-sharing does not have a detrimental effect upon the education of children, otherwise the Council would not have introduced such a scheme. The tribunal held that the imposition of the condition was not justifiable.

In *Tickle*,[27] a part-time teacher did not have her fixed-term contract renewed because the school wanted a full-time worker. This was held to be indirect discrimination. Although the head teacher said that there had been complaints about the fact that children were being taught by two people, the applicant had not been informed of these complaints. The tribunal found that the main reason for the contract not being renewed was financial rather than the emotional and educational needs of the children.

One school's OFSTED report said that pupils received good quality education as a result of the detailed record-keeping, shared planning and ongoing communication carried out by two job-sharing teachers.[28]

In *Eley*,[29] the employer refused to allow a woman receptionist to work part-time. She was the 'shop window' to any visitors and the hub around which enquiry activity from customers would revolve. She was required to be familiar with the product, in this case ultrasound instruments, in order to refer calls to the appropriate department. Seventy per cent of the enquiries about sales were from customers and it was known that a customer ringing in the morning would prefer to deal with the same person if there had to be a referral later in the day. The employer also said that her absence was 'disastrous' for the company. The tribunal held that the requirement to work full-time was justified.

This decision was influenced by the fact that the company relied on telesales and the receptionist provided a vital role. The decision might have been different if the company had been able to provide adequate cover for Ms Eley's absences, if the company had not largely been concerned with telesales, or if personal knowledge of the customers was not so important because, for example, everything was computerised.

In *Todd*,[30] a housing officer was not allowed to return to work on a job-share. The manager argued the importance of continuity in dealing with individual members of the public. However, the manager himself had introduced a team system to avoid the problem of housing officers absent because of holidays or sickness and cases getting lost, and he saw it as a more efficient way of using his manpower resources. The tribunal said the introduction of a team system knocked on the head the argument that the general public would be affected if job-sharing was introduced.

Continuity may be achieved by each employee working for part of every day, though this will increase the employee's travel to work time. In *Carey*,[31] the EAT held that it was reasonable to insist that the applicant, a health visitor, be present for half a day every day in order to provide continuity and it was justifiable to refuse to allow her to work a three-day week.

g But everyone will want to do it: flexible working hours are an undesirable precedent

In *Wright*,[32] the applicant, a single parent, wanted to take half an hour for lunch and leave work half an hour earlier in order to collect her child. The Council argued this would affect their flexi-time policy and set an undesirable precedent. The tribunal rejected this defence.

h We are at saturation point

In *Quarterly*,[33] the employer argued that there were so many part-time factory workers they had reached saturation point as it caused serious capacity problems affecting the day-to-day running of the business. One of the stated problems was that there were too many different starting and finishing times. However, the tribunal was not convinced by this as the same problem applied to the full-time workers.

i Working long hours is a necessary requirement for leadership and motivation of junior staff

In *Robinson*,[34] a tribunal held that a term in a branch manager's contract requiring her to work 'such hours as may be necessary' over and above her standard working week was indirectly discriminatory. The applicant usually had to work a 50 hour week. She asked if she could work fixed hours on her return from maternity leave so that she could arrange child-care. This would involve her job being filled by herself and another person on a job-share basis.

The employers argued that it was necessary for one person to do the job and it would not be possible to have fixed hours and thus have a job-share; the post required leadership and motivation of the junior staff, recruitment, and responsibility for stock control and the general running of the business.

The tribunal heard evidence from New Ways to Work to the effect that:

▶ employers are suspicious of job-share schemes, until the advantages of retaining qualified staff and motivating the work force are explained to them;

▶ a job-share will not necessarily mean any additional costs or any lack of motivation generally in the work force;

▶ very senior jobs have been job-shared, including the Chief Executive of an NHS Trust, and a ward sister's post in a busy London hospital;

▶ deputy managers at Boots, who are responsible for many more staff than those at Oddbins, have been successfully job-sharing.

The tribunal held that the employers had failed to justify the condition, and had not considered the job-share option properly or with an open mind.

j   The employee is not suitable

The employer may argue that an employee is not suitable because, for example, she is unreliable. This should not be a good reason if the employee is unreliable because she needs to take time off for child-care reasons, the alleged unreliability is likely to be resolved by allowing her to work part-time. If in doubt the employer could agree a trial period.

k   Offer of alternative part-time job

The offer of an alternative job on a part-time basis is not good enough. In *Clay*,[36] a teacher was not allowed to return to work as a job-share but was offered an alternative part-time job. The tribunal held that although the introduction of a job-sharing scheme causes considerable logistical problems so far as the employer is concerned, there was no evidence that it could be detrimental to the educational interests of the school. The applicant was entitled to return to her old job on a part-time basis. However, in

Gill,[37] the tribunal held that the employer's decision to demote two mid-wives when they returned to work part-time was justifiable. Their original higher grade entailed ongoing responsibility for patients even when off duty and they had responsibility for supervising junior staff.

Footnotes

[1] *Bilka-Kaufhaus GmbH v Weber von Hartz* [1986] IRLR 317 see also Gerster v Freistaad Bayern [1997] IRLR 699 ECJ.

[2] *Hill v Revenue Commissioners* [1998] IRLR 466.

[3] *London Underground v Edwards* (no 2) [1997] IRLR 157, EAT.

[4] *Jones v Chief Adjudication Office* [1990] IRLR 533.

[5] *Hampson v Department of Department of Education and Science* [1989] IRLR 69 CA.

[6] *R v Secretary of State for Employment ex parte EOC* [1994] IRLR 176, HL.

[7] *United Distillers v Gordon* EAT.12.97 Edinburgh IT.

[8] See footnote 6.

[9] *Rinner-Kuhn v FWW Spezial-Gebaudereinigung GmbH* [1989] IRLR 493, ECJ.

[10] *Nimz v Freie und Hansestadt* Hamburg [1991] IRLR 222.

[11] *R v Secretary of State for Employment exp Seymour Smith* [1995] IRLR 464, CA.

[12] *Barret v Newport BC*, Case No. 340 96/91.

[13] *Stimpson v Dewjoc Partnership* Case No. 61562/94.

[14] See footnote 12.

[15] *Hicks v North Yorkshire County Council* CC COIT 1643/117.

[16] *Watt v Ballantyne and Copeland* Case No: s/1262/94.

[17] See *Change at the Top : Working flexibly at senior and managerial levels in organisations*, New Ways to Work (1993).

[18] *Given v Scottish Power plc* Case No. S/3172/94; Glasgow IT 20.1.95.

[19] *Quarterly v Welwyn Lighting Designs Ltd* Case No. 24781/96 London North 14.8.96.

[20] *Squillaci v W S Atkins (Services) Ltd* Case No. 68108/94 London South 21.1.97.

[21] *Home Office v Holmes* [1984] IRLR 299.

[22] *Cheal and Walker v Sussex Alcohol Advice Service* Case Nos. 34889/94 & 36691/94 23.2.95.

[23] See footnote 13.

[24] See footnote 12.

[25] See footnote 20.

[26] *Clay v The Governors, English Martyrs School* [1993] Case No. 52319/91, Leicester IT 8.1.93.

[27] *Tickle v Governors of Riverview of School and Surrey County Council* COIT Case No. 32420/92 London South, 24.8.93 and 8.7.94.

[28] NUT *Equality Bulletin* March 1997.

[29] *Eley v Huntleigh Diagnostics Ltd.* Case No. 20582/96 Cardiff IT

[30] *Todd v Rushcliffe BC* 11339/90 Nottingham IT 1.2.91.

[31] *Greater Glasgow Health Board v Carey* [1987] IRLR 484.

[32] *Wright v Rugby Borough Council* Case No. 23528/84.

[33] See footnote 19.

[34] *Robinson v Oddbins Ltd* Case No. 4225/95 EAT 188/96.

[35] *Gold v London Borough of Tower Hamlets* Case No. 05608/91/LN/C London North 9.12.91.

[36] See footnote 26.

[37] *Gill and Oakes v Wirral Health Authority* Case Nos. 16165 – 6/90.

Chapter 7

Discrimination against part-timers

Achieving part-time hours can be just the beginning, not the end, of problems for women. Here again the law can help. Women (and men) who change to part-time work need to be aware of the consequences of reduced hours, for example how their pay, benefits, pension and redundancy rights may be affected. Entitlement to benefits, such as family credit and the new working families tax credit will also need to be taken into account, but this is outside the scope of this book.

Many employers acknowledge the benefits of child-friendly working hours, including part-time work. Others do not. Over half of part-time workers feel that employers see them as 'second class staff'. Common reactions are that part-time workers are 'less committed to the job', they are 'not properly integrated' and 'their priorities are elsewhere'.[1]

These negative assumptions about part-timers are based on little more than prejudice and are discriminatory. They need to be challenged through negotiation and, if necessary, the law. Part-time workers should have the same rights, pay and terms and conditions, as full-timers, but on a pro rata basis. So, for example, if a full-time worker gets 30 days holiday, a person working half the number of hours should get 15 days.

1 How to make a claim for pro rata rights and benefits

Less favourable treatment of part-time workers will, in many situations, be unlawful sex discrimination under either UK and/or EC law.[2]

Making a claim: which Act?

Where the claim relates to a matter in the contract, such as pay or other contractual terms, it must be brought under the Equal Pay Act (EqPA)

Where it relates to a non-contractual matter, such as allocation of work, access to promotion, training, transfers, the claim will be under the Sex Discrimination Act (SDA).

If there is any doubt about whether a claim should be made under the EqPA or SDA, it is advisable to make the claim under both – as well as EC law – Article 119 of the Treaty of Rome (see p122).

Remember

Part-time workers, irrespective of the hours they work, are now entitled to the same statutory employment rights as full-time workers, including, for example, protection from unfair dismissal, entitlement to redundancy, and entitlement to a written statement of terms and conditions.[3]

2 Contractual claims

The details of the equal pay legislation and Article 119 are outside the scope of this guide.[4] The following is a brief summary.

What are pay and contractual rights?

Pay is widely defined to include wages and salary, maternity pay, payments towards an occupational pension scheme, contractual and statutory sick pay, redundancy pay, payments for time off for union duties, compensation for unfair dismissal, other perks payable by the employer as a result of the employee's employment.

Contractual rights may be set out in a written or oral contract. They may also be contained in policies and procedures. Local authorities, for example, have a 'Green Book' which sets out the rights of local government employees.

Proving a case under EqPA

The EqPA covers pay and other contractual terms, provided there is a comparable man. Under the EqPA, the woman must show that she is doing like work (the same or similar job); or work rated as equivalent under a job evaluation scheme; or work of equal value; (usually proved by relying on an expert's report) with a comparable man in the same employment. The woman will be entitled to the same terms and conditions as her comparator unless the employer can show there is a 'material factor' defence, which must not be a difference of sex.

One problem which frequently arises is that there is no man doing like work, work rated as equivalent or work of equal value. It is then very difficult to bring a claim under the EqPA.[5]

The material factor defence

The employer will have a defence if s/he can show that there is a material factor which justifies the difference in pay. This may be, for example, that the employee has substantially more experience which results in a higher standard of work.

The defence must not be tainted by discrimination. If the reason for paying the woman less, or denying her equivalent benefits is because she is part-time, this will be indirect discrimination and the employer will have to justify it in the same way as under the SDA (see Chapter 6).[6]

The EOC Code of Practice on Equal Pay

Para 23: Where pay benefits, such as occupational pensions or sick pay, are available only to full-time employees, this rule may mean that a group of female employees, ie those who work part-time, are denied access to important benefits.

Para 33: A smaller percentage of women than men are covered by the organisation's sick pay, pensions, lower interest loans, share option schemes.

Recommended action for employers

Check eligibility requirements. Are there restrictions which impact negatively on women? For example, are any of these limited to employees working over a minimum number of hours? Can these requirements be justified objectively?

---

3 Different types of pay and contractual benefits

A part-time worker should be paid the same hourly rate as a full-time worker.[7] In addition to receiving the same pay, part-time workers should receive the same pro rata contractual benefits.

a Overtime

Overtime rates are usually paid when employees work more than their contractual hours. The question is whether part-time employees are entitled to overtime when they have worked more than **their** normal hours.

The ECJ, in *Helmig*,[8] decided that there was no breach of European law where overtime was only paid for hours worked in excess of the normal full-time working hours. Thus, part-time workers were not entitled to overtime supplements when they exceeded **their** normal working hours, only when they worked more than the normal hours for full-timers. This was because the overall pay of full-timers and part-timers was the same for the same number of hours worked. This decision of the ECJ is likely to be followed by UK courts and tribunals.

b Antisocial hours and call out payments

It is quite common for part-time workers to be excluded from antisocial hours payments. These are payments made for working early in the morning, late at night, shift working and other irregular hours. Part-time workers should receive antisocial hours payments in the same way as full-time workers.

For example

The employment of a shift of part time workers in the evening to supplement the full-time workforce is common in manufacturing. Most of the part-timers are woman but the unsocial hours premium available to other shift workers is rarely paid. A Labour Research Department survey found that amongst 21 examples of twilight shifts, all predominantly or exclusively worked by women, only three paid shift premiums over and above the hourly rate.[9] If such payments are made to employees employed on equal work (see p71), part-time workers should also be entitled to them.

The EOC Code of Practice on Equal Pay

Para 29: A smaller percentage of women employees receive enhanced rates for weekend and unsocial hours work.

Recommended action for employers

Check the eligibility requirements for this work. Do any of these, for example, require that employees must be working full-time, work to the disadvantage of women? Can these requirements be objectively justified?

---

c   Seniority and service-related payments

The aim of these payments is generally to reward the increased experience of long standing members of staff and to reduce staff turnover. Some employers require longer service from part-time workers. This will be discriminatory unless the employer can show that there is a relationship between the duties performed and the experience gained by working the extra hours (see also p78).

Case example
Full-time workers are automatically entitled to be upgraded after six years service, while part-time workers have to wait 12 years. In *Nimz*,[10] the European Court held that this was discriminatory unless the employer could show a link between longer hours and greater experience (see also *Hill*).[11]

d   Productivity and performance related pay

The MSF union for staff in the finance sector found that part-time staff are rarely rated anything other than 'average' or 'effective'.

Part-time workers should be entitled to the same pro rata productivity pay, profit related pay and bonuses as full-time workers. If it is possible to establish a clear pattern of lower performance-related pay to part-time workers (for example, by asking questions under the questionnaire procedure), it should be possible to challenge this as discriminatory. In *Danfoss*,[12] the employer paid the same basic pay but additional payments were made for 'flexibility' which resulted in lower pay for women. The ECJ held that criteria relating to the quality of work which systematically discriminated against women were automatically unfair as, the ECJ pointed out, it was inconceivable that women's work would be of a consistently lower quality than men's.

e   Other payments

The same principles, that part-timers should receive pro rata rights, apply to:
- flexibility payments (for flexible working),
- call out payments (paid for being called out outside work hours),
- attendance allowances (paid for good attendance),
- location allowances,
- labour market supplements,

- ▶ working conditions payments (where working conditions are poor),
- ▶ mobility payments (for being mobile).

f Sick pay

Part-time workers should receive the same pro rata contractual sick pay as full-time workers.[13]

g Pension entitlement

It used to be common for part-time workers to be excluded from access to the employer's pension scheme. This has been successfully challenged on a number of occasions.[14] Exclusion of part-time workers from the pension scheme is likely to be unlawful discrimination. Part-time workers who have not been allowed to join a pension scheme over previous years are entitled to full membership of the pension scheme, and to additional backdated benefits.

The Equal Pay Act S2(5) limits a claim for backdated pay to the two years immediately before the issue of the proceedings. In Magorrian,[15] the European Court held that the two year limit is a breach of EC law and an individual entitled to access to a pension scheme should be able to receive the benefits back to 1976, the date of the decision in Bilka.[16] However, because of the special circumstances of this case a fuller reference has been made in Preston, to decide whether the two year limitation is a breach of EC law.[17] Note, however, that a woman claiming the benefit, must also contribute her share over the same period, see Fisscher.[18]

There are different methods of calculating the pension entitlement of part-time workers. Usually the part-time work is translated into the full-time equivalent. Thus, if a woman works 18 hours (instead of 36), after four years her pension will be based on two years' full-time service.

h Redundancy payments

Statutory redundancy pay is calculated according to the number of years service of the employee and existing pay, subject to a weekly maximum.

Redundancy payments are based on the employee's salary at the time she is made redundant, even if she previously earned much more by working longer hours. Many employers offer more favourable contractual redundancy terms, based on longer years or without a limit on the weekly pay. The same calculation is usually adopted. The Court of Appeal in *Barry*,[19] have held that the method of calculation is not discriminatory.

For example

If a woman worked full-time for ten years on a salary of between £18,000 and £20,000, but recently changed to part-time work on a salary of £15,000, her redundancy payment would be based on the salary of £15,000. This is the case even though all her years of service are taken into account. Her existing lower rate of pay is the basis for the calculation of the redundancy payment.

Case example

Mrs Barry was employed full-time for eleven years, then took maternity leave and returned to work on $17^1/2$ hours per week. She took voluntary redundancy three years later and made a complaint that her full-time years and salary should be taken into account in calculating the redundancy payment.

The Court of Appeal held that there was no discrimination because:

a   Mrs Barry could not show that there was adverse impact as there were no statistics about the number of part-time and full-time men and women in the relevant pool;

b   The method of calculation was justified because the scheme could not be redrafted without detracting from its main aim to cushion the effect of unemployment. It also had the merit of being clear and simple. Administrative convenience was a legitimate aim.

i   Holidays

An estimated one third of employees working fewer than 20 hours a week are not entitled to any paid holidays.[20] Part-time workers should receive the same holidays pro rata as full-time workers; refusal to give holidays pro rata may be in breach of the Equal Pay Act and/or Article 119.

Where a bank holiday falls on a day when a part-timer does not generally work (often a Monday), arguably she should receive time off pro rata. This may be worked out over the period of a year.

The Working Time Regulations give most workers at least four weeks paid holiday a year (see p124).

j   Paid time off for trades union duties

What happens if a part-time trades union official has to attend a work-related training course which exceeds her normal working hours? In *Botel*,[21] the European Court held that she should be paid for the full hours. The applicant attended a training course as a member of the staff committee (which is similar to a trades union). German law provided that she was entitled to be released from work without a reduction in salary if necessary to perform her duties. The European Court held that part-timers were treated less favourably than full-time committee members because they were not paid as the training took place outside **their** normal working hours although within the normal working hours of full-time workers. Because the part-time workers were generally women such treatment was indirect discrimination. They were therefore entitled to full-time pay.

In *Kuratorium*,[22] a similar decision was reached. However, in *Nazir*,[23] attendance at a trades union annual conference was found not to be 'work'; this is arguably wrong and inconsistent with *Botel*.

k   Paid time off for training

Similar principles to those in *Botel* should apply to other training. If part-time workers have to attend training courses for a full-time week, they should receive the same pay for that week as the full-time workers.

A more difficult issue is the ability of a part-time worker to attend a course which is full-time. Access to training is covered on p78.

Note
Entitlement to benefits should be based on the actual hours worked, as opposed to just the contractual hours.

4 Non-contractual matters

The Equal Pay Act deals only with matters contained in the contract of employment. Non-contractual claims are generally covered by the Sex Discrimination Act,[24] which prohibits discrimination in access to benefits, facilities or services (see p119).

a   Access to promotion

Employees are often told that if they change to part-time work, it will harm their promotion prospects. If this is the case, it may well be discriminatory if the employer cannot justify it.

Case example

In *Gold*,[25] the tribunal found that a solicitor was not promoted because she was job-sharing. The tribunal said that the respondents, a local authority, 'paid lip service to the equal opportunities policy' when they advertised the job on a job-share basis. The applicant had done the job on a temporary basis but had been told it would not be permanent because she was a job-sharer. There were no good reasons for the council's failure to put her forward to the final panel. She won her claim for indirect discrimination and was awarded £6,000 for injury to feelings.

Where promotion is linked to length of service and part-timers length of service is not treated in the same way as full-timers, this may be discriminatory if the employer cannot justify it.

Case example

In *Gerster*,[26] the applicant worked part time, for half normal working hours. She applied for promotion, which was based on merit and length of service. Regulations provided that periods of employment where the employee's hours were less than half normal working hours were not taken into account when calculating length of service. Periods of employment during which the hours worked were at least half normal working hours were treated as equivalent to two-thirds. Ms Gerster asked for her part-time employment to be treated as full-time but was refused and she was not promoted.

The ECJ held that where part-time employees accrue length of service more slowly, and so take longer to achieve promotion, this is a breach of the Equal Treatment Directive, unless the employer can justify this. The employer would need to show a link between length of service and acquisition of a certain level of knowledge or experience, for example that:

▶ part-time employees are generally slower than full-time employees in acquiring job-related abilities and skills;

▶ the provisions reflect, in the case of legislation, a legitimate social policy aim and

▶ they are an appropriate means of achieving the policy aim.

b Length of service treated differently

The decision in *Gerster* would apply to other situations where the service of part-timers is treated as shorter than equivalent time worked by full-timers. In *Kording*,[27] German legislation provided that the total length of professional experience required for exemption from a qualifying examination was to be extended on a pro rata basis for part-time workers. This gave rise to indirect discrimination against women if substantially fewer men than women worked part time. It might be justified if the requirement to work the longer period could be shown to lead to greater experience.

In *Hill*, two women, who had been job-sharing moved to full-time work. They were told that two years' job-sharing service should be counted as one year's full time service so they lost out on annual increments. It was accepted that a job-sharer could acquire the same experience as a full-time worker. The only difference being in the time actually worked. The ECJ held that the assessment of incremental credit (based on service) had a disparate impact and the employers had to justify it. However, neither a generalised assertion nor costs reasons were sufficient to show justification (see also p58 and p64).

c Access to training

Part-time workers are less likely to receive training than full-timers. The Labour Force Survey (Winter 1993-94) shows that about 11% of all part-time workers had some job-related training in the four weeks before the survey compared with 18% of full-time workers. Part-time workers should have access to training in the same way as full-time workers. Arguably, employers should also attempt to arrange training at a time when the part-timer works. However, this may not be possible if there are a number of part-timers working at different times and it will depend on the circumstances.

> **The EOC Code of Practice**
> **Para 43:** Where residential training is necessary, staff selected should be informed well in advance to enable them to make child-care and other personal arrangements; employers with residential training centres could also consider whether childcare facilities might be provided.

d   Selection for redundancy

It will usually be unlawful indirect discrimination to adopt a selection method whereby part-time workers are made redundant before full-time workers.[28] Where a woman is made redundant while on maternity leave or absence, she is entitled to be offered suitable alternative employment (see p135). She should also be consulted – even if she is on maternity leave.

e   Allocation of work

A woman who works part-time should not be given less favourable work unless the employer can justify this. To do so will be discriminatory. The more flexible the woman can be, for example, being available for emergencies or in exceptional circumstances, the harder it will be for the employer to justify the less favourable allocation of work. (see p86).

5 Statutory provisions

Lower earnings limit for national insurance

Employees earning less than the lower earnings limit are not entitled to statutory sick pay or statutory maternity pay. The vast majority of those who are not entitled work part-time and are women. Denial of SSP is arguably indirectly discriminatory on grounds of sex. Failure to pay SMP to women who are not entitled to it is also being challenged.[29]

Footnotes

[1] *Part-time workers: a guide to negotiation and recruitment* LRD and TUC (1996)

[2] *Bilka-Kaufhaus GmbH v Weber von Hartz* [1986] IRLR 317.

[3] *R v Secretary of State for Employment ex parte EOC* [1994] IRLR 176 where the House of Lords held that the minimum hours qualification requirements were indirectly discriminatory against women. See Employment Protection (Part-Time Employees) Regulations 1995 SI No 31.

[4] See *Discrimination at Work* Palmer C, Moon G and Cox S, LAG (1997).

[5] There may still be a claim under EC Article 119, but specialist legal advice should be sought.

[6] EqPA s1(3). The law on this is complicated. It is difficult to envisage many factors on which an employer could rely to justify not giving pro rata benefits to part-time workers.

[7] EqPA 1970, s1.

[8] *Stadt Lengerich v Helmig* [1995] IRLR 216, ECJ.

[9] Part time workers: LRD (1994).

[10] *Nimz v Freie und Hansestadt* Hamburg [1991] IRLR 222.

[11] *Hill and Stapleton v Revenue Commissioners and Department of Finance* [1998] IRLR 466.

[12] *Handels-og Kontorfunktionaerernes Forbund i Danmark v Dansk Arbejdsgiverforening* (acting for Danfoss) [1989] IRLR 532, ECJ.

[13] *Rinner-Kuhn v FWW Spezial-Gebaudereinigung GmbH* [1989] IRLR 493, ECJ.

[14] *Bilka KaufhausGmbH v Weber von Hartz* [1986] IRLR 317, ECJ, *Vroege v NCIV Instituut voor Volkshuisvesting BV* [1994] IRLR 651, ECJ.

[15] *Magorrian and Cunningham v Eastern Health and Social Services Board and Department of Health and Social Services* [1998] IRLR 86 ECJ.

[16] See footnote 2.

[17] *Preston and others v Wolverhampton Healthcare NHS Trust* [1998] IRLR 197.

[18] *Fisscher v Voorhuis Hengelo BV* [1994] IRLR 662, ECJ.

[19] *Barry v Midland Bank plc* [1998] IRLR 138 CA. It is on appeal to the HL.

[20] See footnote 1.

[21] *Arbeiterwohlfahrt der Stadt Berlin eV v Botel* [1992] IRLR 423, ECJ

[22] *Kuratorium Fur Dialyse and Neirentransplantation eV v Lewark* [1996] IRLR 637.

[23] *Manor Bakeries Ltd v Nazir* [1996] IRLR 604.

[24] SDA s6(1)(b), 6(2)(a). For details of difference between SDA and EqPA see: *Discrimination at Work,* Palmer C, Moon G and Cox S, LAG (1997).

[25] *Gold v London Borough of Tower Hamlets* [1991], Case No. 05608/91/LN/C.

[26] *Gerster v Freistaat Bayern* (C-1/95) [1997] IRLR 700. A similar case in the UK would be brought under the SDA as the promotion was not a contractual right (unlike the case of *Nimz*)

[27] *Kording v Senator fun Finanzen* [1997] IRLR 710.

[28] *Clarke v Eley Kynock Ltd* [1982] IRLR 482. Note that the EAT said that a dismissal which is indirectly discriminatory is also likely to be unfair.

[29] *Banks v Tesco and Secretary of State for Employment* 18985/95 Ashford IT. To be heard by EAT early 1999.

Chapter 8

The case for child-friendly working hours

To achieve working hours that fit childcare responsibilities, firstly a woman must consider her preferred option and what she is prepared to accept – her top and bottom line. For some women, the right to go to an employment tribunal and the remedy, generally compensation, may be inadequate compensation for the loss of a job.

Secondly, the woman should be clear from the outset why she cannot work full-time or the required hours and should, at the appropriate time, tell her employer. Her reasons may be related to:

▶ childcare (availability and cost);
▶ particular problems of the children (health or behavioural),
▶ the stress of combining long hours at work with childcare,
▶ the absence of a partner to share childcare responsibilities (see Chapter 5).

Thirdly, the woman needs to consider whether and how the job can be done on different hours; the employer will need to be persuaded that the job can be done on child-friendly hours.

Finally, the woman will have to consider the employer's likely response and decide how to respond to it.

Remember

▶ if a woman successfully negotiates part-time work, there is no right to return to full-time work later; however, it may be possible to agree reduced hours for a limited period only (but see p95);
▶ it is important, if possible, for women to return to the **same** job, but on child-friendly hours (see p131ff). Some employers offer part-time work on a different basis, for example, in a lower status job, on a self-employed basis or on the condition that there is a new contract and no continuity of service. Whether a woman is prepared to accept a change in terms and conditions may well depend on how

far she is prepared to enforce her legal rights and whether she can afford to resign if refused a change in hours.

1 The employer's attitude

The employer's attitude is crucial. It may influence how and when negotiations are carried out. An employer who has been hostile to the woman's pregnancy and to flexible working generally is less likely to agree to a change in hours. If this is the case the woman must consider:

▶ whether she wants to return to the same job on the same hours, or
▶ whether she will accept a proposal (if there is one) to work part-time but on a less favourable basis, and/or
▶ whether she is willing to take legal proceedings.

2 What to find out and consider

It is important to collect evidence about whether and how other jobs have been done on child-friendly hours – preferably in the same workplace. This is important in order to find out the employer's attitude and persuade her/him that the job **can** be done on such hours. Relevant information could be:

▶ Has the same or a similar job been done on a part-time or job-share basis previously? If so, did it work and, if not, why not?
▶ Do other employees work part-time or job-share or have other flexible working arrangements? If so, have there been any problems and are they treated in the same way as full-timers?
▶ Have other employees asked to work part-time or to job-share? What happened to their request? What reasons were given if they were refused.
▶ Is there an equal opportunities or maternity policy relating to reduced or flexible hours? If there is such a policy there is a stronger argument that an employee should be allowed to job-share (see p61). Some policies say that applications for job-sharing will be considered in relation to each job. Others say that all jobs can be job-shared unless they are exempted. It is important to check the policy. Those working for schools or other local authority run bodies

should check if the local authority has a policy.

▶ If the job was shared, how would it work in practice? Would the work be shared or divided equally between job-sharers? What system would there be for overlap? For suggestions about how to deal with practical problems see p97ff;

▶ What objections is the employer likely to make and how would these be overcome (for details, see Chapter 6)?

Remember

If there is a trades union prepared to negotiate on behalf of individual employees, this is usually the best option. This should reduce the potential conflict between employer and employee.

The questionnaire can be used to ask some of the questions in 2 above.

3 Who to ask

If the line manager is approachable and sympathetic, it is best to approach him or her first. If not, and there is a personnel department, it may be better to talk to them and find out about the organisation's views.

4 When to ask

Some women are unsure what they want and prefer to wait until after the baby is born. It is better not to wait until just before returning to work as this may make it more difficult for the employer to accommodate a request, particularly if it is necessary to re-arrange the work or appoint another worker to do the remaining hours.

Other women know as soon as they are pregnant that they want to return part-time. It is in both the employee's and the employer's interests to try and agree at an early stage as it will leave more time to negotiate and give the employer the opportunity to make appropriate arrangements. It may affect the choice of maternity replacement and how the work is organised in the woman's absence.

Even if the employer refuses the request before the woman goes on maternity leave, she can ask again on her return. However, there is a danger that, if the employer confirms the previous decision without reconsidering it, the woman will be out of time for bringing a claim – unless there has been and still is a continuing policy not to allow part-time work (see p145).

Note

If there is a grievance procedure the employee should usually take out a grievance. This should ensure that the request is properly considered. However, the woman should not miss the time limit.

5 What to request

All forms of child-friendly working, which would be compatible with the particular job in question and the needs of the woman, should be considered, for example:

a   **Part-time working:** this is the most common form of child-friendly working. It can involve any number of hours. Although the Labour Force Survey definition of 'part-time' work is less than 30 hours per week, it can be more than this where the normal weekly hours are higher, or as low as two. Part-timers should received pro rata rights and benefits (see Chapter 7);

b   **Job-sharing:** this is where one job is shared between two employees, usually on a 50/50 basis (for example, two and a half days each) but it may be a different split (eg two days/three days). Duties, responsibilities, pay and benefits are split;

c   **Flexible hours:** the employer has some choice over the hours worked. It can take many forms, but is usually limited by 'core' hours such as from 11am to 3pm during which time the employee must work. The employee can choose which other hours to work. Some schemes allow an employee to work extra hours on some days and then take one day off every fortnight or month. A woman may only want to have a short lunch break in order to arrive at work or leave earlier, subject to the Working Time Regulations which specify what breaks an employee must take (see p124).

d   School hours and/or term time working: this is less common and such arrangements are only likely to be available in a few jobs, mostly teaching and other education positions.[1] However, Boots the Chemists allows some employees to work term time only. Women wanting to work term time only should get agreement that they have continuous employment to avoid losing employment rights such as protection from unfair dismissal, which at present depend on having been employed continuously for two years.

e   Working from home and teleworking: 'homeworkers', who work exclusively from home and are mainly in the lowest paid jobs, usually do so because they have no choice. However, modern technology has increased the possibility of other jobs being done wholly or partly from home.

f   Shift swopping: this is where employees are allowed to swop shifts between themselves. This enables some flexibility, particularly if there is a family emergency.

Some of these options will not be possible in particular jobs. A check-out operator in a supermarket could not work from home but could job-share or work part-time and may be able to do term time working. Employers could consider employing students in vacation time.

Remember

Employers often say that a job cannot be done on a part-time basis because the work cannot be completed in fewer than full-time hours. If that is the case, the employer should also consider whether the job can be shared by two people on a job-share basis, or, alternatively, whether another employee, part-time or full-time, can do the rest of the work.

6 Negotiating different options

Some women are able to be more adaptable than others, particularly if they have flexible childcare arrangements; if so, this should be made clear to the employer.

For other women, childcare may be quite limited or there may be other limits on hours, for example:

- ▶ many childminders will not work before 8.30am or after 6pm;
- ▶ many women rely on relatives or friends for childcare, either because there is no other suitable childcare or because it is not affordable; this may restrict the woman's hours of work;
- ▶ some women may need to take their child(ren) to nursery or school in the morning or collect them some afternoons;
- ▶ some women cannot afford to work fewer hours but need to adjust their hours to fit in with their childcare.

Although a woman may have a preference for two and a half or three days a week, she may be prepared to work four or even five days a week, provided she can work one or two days from home and work through her lunch hour; this can substantially reduce travelling time and/or time away from home. Another option is to ask for longer holidays or unpaid time off during the school holidays.

Some women, particularly in more senior jobs, where there may be less scope for another employee making a decision, are prepared to offer to go into work if there is an emergency and to be contactable by mobile phone, fax, computer link or e-mail. Again this will depend on childcare arrangements.

The broader the range of options put forward, the easier it is for the woman to deal with objections put forward by the employer and the more difficult it becomes for an employer to justify his/her inflexibility. Thus, an employer may say that a woman cannot work part-time because there may be an emergency in her absence which no-one else could deal with. If she is prepared to be available to advise on how to deal with the emergency, this makes such an objection more difficult to sustain.

Remember

When negotiating on the basis of alternative options, a woman needs to be careful that she does **not** say that she **could** work full-time but **prefers** not to do so. The danger is that if the woman subsequently brings a claim for indirect discrimination, the tribunal will find that she was able to comply with a full-time working requirement, but merely **preferred** to spend more time with her child (see p45).

7 The business case

It is important to point out to employers the advantages to them of child-friendly working hours. There are general advantages common to all child-friendly working hours and specific advantages for different types of work patterns. A policy advisor at the Inland Revenue said:

> *'Any job can be worked on a flexible basis if the will is there. The employer and employee need to understand the needs of the other'.*[2]

The Director General of the CBI, Adair Turner, has said that most managerial jobs, are 'splittable'. An exception, he added, would be the job of Prime Minister.

Evidence that other employers allow their employees, who are doing similar work, to work child-friendly hours may be useful (see p60). If, in relation to a particular job, one employer allows job-sharing, and it works, why should another employer refuse?

There is enormous variation in the provision of different types of child-friendly working arrangements. Employers who offer a range of child-friendly policies, are much more likely to see the provision of child-friendly working arrangements as beneficial to management than those offering fewer arrangements. In a Department for Education and Employment report nine out of ten respondents from model establishments said management gained benefits, compared with just over half of those establishments with a narrower range of provisions.[3]

The survey found that, of establishments at which there was some kind of family-friendly working arrangement, the benefits most commonly mentioned were:

► improved morale/staff relations (50%);
► easier retention of staff (26%);
► enhanced loyalty (25%);
► improved performance/motivation (23%);
► enhanced flexibility (14%).

An IRS survey of 100 organisations found flexible working arrangements to be the most popular and effective of eight measures considered for recruiting and retaining women workers. Thirty-eight per cent said they offered management both benefits and problems. A further 21% said they only offered problems, 17% said they only offered benefits and

10% said they offered neither benefits nor problems. The business case for child-friendly working hours is summarised below, supported by examples from different organisations (see also p90).

a   Increased efficiency, enthusiasm, morale and commitment

Research by the Institute of Manpower Studies (IMS) found that staff working non-standard hours were considered to be 'more efficient, enthusiastic and committed' than full time employees. In 1995 Sir Nicholas Goodison, Chairman of the TSB Group said: 'A culture that values long hours above all else is not only unhealthy for individuals and for families, it is also in the long run damaging to corporate productivity and therefore to shareholders' returns.... Staff who are fulfilled and refreshed must be more productive, better employees.'[6]

b   The competitive edge

'In the 90s, it is the family-friendly employer who will have the competitive edge...If employers are to make the best use of their most valuable resource – the work-force – they will need to ensure the well-being of their employees by enabling them to meet family responsibilities – when children are young, according to Vasso Papandreou, EC Commissioner for Social Affairs in 1992.[7]

c   Attracting and retaining high calibre staff

Child-friendly policies are likely to attract more applicants to jobs and therefore better candidates. The Chairman of the TSB Group has said that 'those companies which were able to help staff effectively to achieve a balance between their work and the other aspects of their family and personal lives would be the ones best able to attract talented and skilled employees'. Shell introduced job-sharing in order to open up the pool of labour from which the company could draw.

Howard Davies, a recent Director General of the CBI, speaking at the launch of the EOC's formal investigation into the British National Training System stressed the CBI's commitment to equality of opportunity for all in the workplace as sound business sense, saying 'We are absolutely behind the objective of a balanced workforce. Companies need the best people available – not just the best of half the population'.

d   Encouraging maternity leave returners

A recent survey found that where women worked for an employer who operated a number of family-friendly working arrangements, 67% returned to work for that employer after maternity leave. This compared to only 44% of women who worked for an employer with no such arrangements.[8]

Some arrangements, such as working at home occasionally, are more commonly available to higher grade employees. On the other hand, one study found that employers have often excluded senior positions from opportunities to work in flexible and alternative ways (such as part-time work and job-sharing) which means that women with childcare commitments find it hard to reach the higher ranks of their profession.[9] However, some employers have introduced a new level of first line management with an option of working part time. In 1993 Sainsburys had over 340 part-time managers.[10] Not surprisingly, child-friendly working arrangements were more commonly offered to and taken up by women than men.

8 The business cost of not providing child-friendly working hours

The cost of being child-unfriendly is often ignored. This may be because the costs are intangible and difficult to quantify. However, there is research which shows that these costs can be quite considerable.

a   Increased sick leave and absenteeism associated with long hours

Among the causes of stress which are likely to lead to illness are conflicting demands between work and home. The Health and Safety Executive estimate that 40 million days per year are lost in the UK due to stress related illnesses. This is an increase of 500% since the mid 1950s.[11] According to the World Labour Report from the International Labour Office the effects of stress at work are thought to cost up to 10% of GNP in Britain.[12]

Fifty three percent of respondents in an Industrial Society survey of 700 companies said that stress had increased over the previous three years and led to increased absenteeism (cited by 76%), decreased productivity (cited by 70%), poor judgement and quality (cited by 54%), poor customer care (cited by 41%), high staff turnover (cited by 31%), and accidents (cited by 30%).[13]

b Costs of recruiting and training new staff

When a skilled employee leaves her job, the replacement costs include recruitment and training and a period of reduced work performance while the new employee is being trained. The total cost of employing a junior manager (earning £15,000) has been calculated to be about £7,000. Boots the Chemists has calculated that a one per cent turnover in staff is equivalent to a loss of a million pounds worth of sales.[14]

Rank Xerox has offered flexible working for mothers over the last five years. They reckon that they have saved £1 million on training, recruitment and lost productivity.

Note
Commonly perceived problems, such as the extra administrative burden, inconvenience, lack of continuity, unsuitability of such arrangements to the business, as well as increased costs are discussed in detail in Chapter 6.

Remember the Government's view
The Fairness at Work White Paper says:
'Helping employees to combine work and family life satisfactorily is good not only for parents and children but also for business. Many successful modern companies, both large and small, have therefore adopted culture and practices in support of the family. To the mutual benefit of the employee and the business, they allow flexibility over hours and working from home.

In addition to measures to improve family incomes, the Government's two main priorities are to tackle excessively long working hours and to give parents greater flexibility.'

9 Advantages of different types of child-friendly working

Most of the general advantages apply to each form of child-friendly working. The following are specific advantages.

a   Part-time work and job-sharing

An IDS study found that many employers believe that job-sharing leads to:
- higher motivation and commitment;
- enhanced productivity;
- improved cover for absence or peaks in workload;
- better continuity, because there is less absence for domestic reasons and the impact of sickness absence is halved;
- a wider range of skills and experience is brought to the post – often referred to as 'two for the price of one';
- lower turnover of staff;
- a significant improvement in work effectiveness and efficiency by combining the skills and experience of the job-share partners.[15]

The EC Childcare Guide states:
> *'Hours can be reduced by part-time working, by (temporarily) reduced working hours and by job-share. Part-time working has historically been an option taken up by women and characterised by low pay and low status. Job-share schemes are a more recent development and are less widely available, but generally carry better terms and conditions of employment than part-time work. It is not common yet for either option to be available at professional and managerial levels, although there is, in practice, little reason why this should be so.'*[16]

b   Flexible working

Advantages of flexible working include:
- enabling the employer to provide cover over a longer period;
- reduction of punctuality problems and absence rates;
- improved time management.[17]

The EC Childcare Guide states:
> *'Hours can be staggered by shiftwork or flexi-time. These options can include a very wide range of possibilities – term time working, weekly shifts, three or four day weeks, weekly/monthly/annual balancing hours. Family needs are often as unpredictable as they are unavoidable; a sudden illness or accident involving a child or a carer does not necessarily require a parent to be present the whole day but requires that workers are able to react quickly in emergencies. Flexibility* **within** *the agreed work schedule is the ideal approach in these situations.'*

c Teleworking

Modern technology has increased the possibility of some jobs being done wholly or mainly from home. The disadvantage is that it can be isolating and a combination of working from home and office is often preferable.

More senior jobs which are particularly suited to working from home are those which involve:

▶ a high degree of cerebral, rather than manual work;
▶ work done as an individual, or with clearly defined areas of individual work;
▶ a fair amount of initiative, with teleworkers given objectives and left to work with minimal supervision;
▶ measurable outputs;
▶ no very bulky or costly items of equipment.

An ILO study of teleworking found that employers mentioned the following benefits:

▶ reduction of expenditure on office space (which more than compensates for equipment costs for teleworkers);
▶ increased productivity, due to lack of interruptions and improved concentration;
▶ increased motivation and job satisfaction, higher morale and an increased energy level due to the elimination of commuting.[18]

The Department of Education and Employment encourages managers to examine the teleworking option because:

▶ it widens the range of choice for individuals and business;
▶ it enhances flexibility in working time and methods;
▶ it gives more people the opportunity to work;
▶ it can create jobs in remote areas;
▶ it can help British businesses maintain their competitiveness.[19]

They set out reasons for introducing teleworking. They include:

▶ to retain staff who want to spend more time caring for their families;
▶ to attract staff with disabilities;
▶ to attract or retain people with scarce skills;
▶ to avoid moving to larger premises;
▶ to reduce the amount of time which mobile workers have to spend 'touching base' at the office.

Advantages of teleworking for employees

▶ more time for childcare;
▶ less stress, better health and reduced sickness;
▶ more energy for the job and therefore higher productivity;
▶ with job-sharers there are two sets of skills and knowledge which can benefit each other;
▶ continuity during sickness, holiday or maternity leave.

The EC Childcare Guide says:

> *'Many jobs, and their number is increasing, can be carried out* **in the home**. *The most successful systems seem to be those in which work done at home is combined with regular contacts with the parent workplace or a network of other home workers, to avoid too great a sense of isolation. Flexiplace arrangements can be combined with flexible hours to create an extremely creative response to reconciling work and family responsibilities.'*

Remember

Homeworkers may be employees and therefore protected from unfair dismissal. If not, they will generally be covered by the Sex Discrimination Act which covers a wider category of workers including the self-employed, agency workers, and contract workers (see p116).

A woman who was in the workplace and now works from home should retain her former employment status.

d   Career breaks and sabbaticals

The DfEE study found that 17% of establishments offered career breaks which could be taken for family reasons. A career break was defined as a minimum of three months unpaid time off work after which the employee may return to the same job.

Some local authorities allow women a career break after the birth. Thus, after the end of maternity leave the woman may be able to choose to take a period of unpaid leave. This may be up to five years or longer. Generally, the woman's return to work is dependent on there being a suitable job and she may be required to take no other work during her career break. Some career breaks require resignation with no absolute guarantee of re-engagement, simply a 'hope' of being able to find work. The Parental Leave Directive, when implemented at the end of 1999, will give all parents a right to three months off while the child is young (see p127)

The EC Childcare Guide says:

> *'Career breaks/sabbaticals are usually for longer periods than parental leave, and may not be tied so specifically to the care of very young children.*
>
> *Rather than prescribing a simple model of these longer term breaks employers when consulting with workers may discover that again, flexibility is the answer...it is important to keep good contacts with the employee in her/his absence through skills updating sessions, regular short periods of work, information on developments in the organisation, and careful re-entry training.'*

Remember

Employers and employees should consider all the alternative forms of child-friendly working. A combination of different forms of child-friendly hours may be the most suitable for all parties.

Footnotes

1 B & Q, Dixons, Thistle Hotels and the Alliance and Leicester Building Society have all introduced term time working.
2 *Change at the Top*, New Ways to Work (1993).
3 *Family-Friendly Working Arrangements in Britain*, Research Report No 16, Department for Education and Employment (1996).
4 *Effective Ways of Recruiting and Retaining Women*, IRS (1990).
5 *Family Friendly Working*, IMS (1992).
6 *Workplace Culture: Long hours high stress?* Report of a Seminar, Women's National Commission (1995).
7 *The Family Friendly Employer: examples from Europe*, Daycare Trust (1992).
8 *Maternity Rights and Benefits in Britain 1996*, Social Security Research Report 67, Callender et al, PSI (1997).
9 *Changing Times, A guide to flexible work patterns for human resource managers*, New Ways to Work (1993).
10 See footnote 2.
11 *The Time Squeeze*, DEMOS (1995).
12 *World Labour Report, Stressed at Work* ILO (1993).
13 *Managing Best Practice*, The Industrial Society (1995).
14 See footnote 9.
15 *Job-sharing*, IDS (1994).
16 EC Recommendation on Childcare 92/241/EEC.
17 See footnote 2.
18 *Teleworking, Conditions of Work Digest*, ILO, Geneva, Vol. 9, No. 1 (1990).
19 *A Manager's Guide to Teleworking*, Ursula Huws DfEE.

Chapter 9

Common problems for employees and employers

When considering and negotiating child-friendly hours, it is important for employees to bear in mind possible problems and be ready to discuss how to overcome them.

1 The need for clear agreement

The employer's initial reaction to a request for shorter hours may be to agree but leave the position vague. The woman may then assume that there will be no problem returning part-time, only to be told later that it is not possible. Depending on the circumstances, there may be a contractual agreement which the woman can then enforce. Alternatively, a tribunal may find that no final agreement had been reached. It is therefore preferable for the position to be confirmed in writing, if possible by the employer. Alternatively, the employee could write, setting out the details of the agreement; failure to reply and deny the existence of such an agreement will be evidence that the employer has agreed.

2 Temporary child-friendly hours

An employee may want to work part-time for a short period, perhaps for three months after the end of maternity leave, and then return to full-time work. Alternatively, an employer may agree to allow part-time working for a short period, but then insist on a return to full-time work.

If temporary part-time work is an option, employer and employee should discuss how long it should last. Although it is particularly difficult working full-time with a young baby, older children are also demanding, particularly when there is more than one child. The employee should think very carefully about when full-time working will be feasible, bearing in mind that school usually finishes at around 3.30pm and there are the long holidays.

The danger of asking to work part-time for a short period is that the tribunal may find that the woman could work full-time, having admitted she could do so after the initial period (see p47). If the reason is in order to be able to breastfeed, this should not apply (see p50).

It is still possible to argue that, if at the end of the temporary period, the woman changes her mind and wants to continue working part-time, it is discriminatory not to allow her to do so. If the arrangement has worked, it will be more difficult for the employer to justify a requirement to revert to the previous hours (eg full-time). On the other hand, if it has not worked – for good objective reasons – the employer will find it easier to justify.

3 Request for reduced hours after return to full-time work

It is possible to ask for a change in hours after a woman has returned full-time and then found it impossible to continue. The woman will have to show she cannot continue with the same hours. However, the longer she continues with the long hours, the harder it will be to show she cannot do them – unless her circumstances have changed (see also p52).

4 A trial period

A reluctant employer may be persuaded to allow an employee to vary her hours for a trial period, on the understanding that if it works, it will be extended. This is not the most satisfactory option because the woman will have to arrange temporary childcare; she may worry that barriers will be put in the way of her making it work and a temporary arrangement will have to be devised to deal with the remaining hours – unless the same hours are to be worked but in a different way, for example, at home.

If the employer insists on a trial period, it may give the woman an opportunity to show that the job can be done on child-friendly hours. Generally, it is advisable to accept a trial period and make every effort to show that the job can be done effectively.

A more satisfactory solution is for the employer to assume that the arrangement will work. If it does not, the employer may be able to terminate it if the job is not being done adequately (see below).

Note
If problems arise, these should be discussed with the employer to try and resolve them. Keep notes of any difficulties that arise and how they were overcome.

5 Problems with job-sharing and how to overcome them

a   What if the job-sharers cannot work together?

The onus is generally on two job-sharing employees to make the arrangement works. If they do not, they risk having the job-share withdrawn. In Deacon,[1] the applicant accepted that job-sharing had not been satisfactory because there were different styles of management and an inability to liaise which led to work not being handed over satisfactorily and deteriorating morale in the office. The tribunal found that the function could be shared but only if the particular job-sharers:

a   agreed to job-share and
b   worked together to ensure continuity of work and good staff morale.

As this did not happen the employer was therefore justified in terminating the job-share. In this situation, each person could compete for the full-time job if they could work the hours. Alternatively, there may be other part-time work available. It will depend on the circumstances. The tribunal may have reached a different decision in *Deacon* if only one job-sharer had been clearly at fault or there had been management failings.

b What if the employer agrees, subject to finding a job-share partner?

The employer may agree to a job-share provided a suitable partner can be found. The employer should be encouraged to discuss this with the employee, who may know of a possible job-share partner. Otherwise the employer should advertise internally and externally.

If a job-share is agreed before the woman goes on maternity leave, there will be plenty of time to recruit a partner. Otherwise, the following should be considered:

▶ the woman may be able to work full-time for a short period;
▶ if the woman returns part-time, there may be another employee who can take over the work or the woman's maternity locum may be able to fill in;
▶ a temporary or agency worker may be appointed for a short period.

If the employer says that the woman must stay at home without pay until the job-sharer is recruited, she will need to consider whether this is an acceptable option or she would rather return full-time, pending finding someone else to do the hours. Alternatively, she could argue that she has been denied her right to return and has been discriminated against; it will then be up to the employer to justify refusing to allow her to return part-time, pending a new appointment.

If it is not possible, after making appropriate efforts, to find a suitable partner, there may be other options, such as varying the hours of work, allowing some working from home, employing casual staff to complete some of the employee's tasks.

c What happens if one job-share partner leaves?

If a job-sharer leaves and the person remaining does not want to work full-time, part of the job should be advertised. The remaining job-sharer should be involved in the interviewing process to try and ensure compatibility between the job-sharers. The evidence is that it is generally not difficult to find another job sharer. If it is not possible to find a replacement, all other options should be considered. If none are possible, the existing employee should be offered alternative part-time work where possible.

d Sharing terms and conditions

The usual arrangement is that each employee works half the week, although this may vary so that one does two days, the other three days, or they do alternate weeks. All terms and conditions should be shared equally, including holidays. Bank holidays should be split pro rata so that the person who never works Monday, for example, does not lose out.

It is quite usual for job-sharers to share a room and desk. This avoids any extra expense being incurred by the employer. If there is agreement for an overlap period, the seating arrangements should be discussed between employer and employee. A company car could be shared, with a handover mid-week. Another alternative is to claim a car allowance which could be split between the sharers. An employer, particularly a small one, would not normally be expected to provide two cars as this would greatly increase the costs of employing job-sharers.

e Practical ways of dealing with communication and continuity

Some disadvantages of job-sharing and part-time work identified by employers are communication problems, attendance at meetings, and lack of continuity. Employees wanting to job-share should consider how these potential problems could be minimised. The following are some ideas of how to deal with problems, although it is impossible to generalise because the needs of the job and the job-sharer will vary so much. Detailed record keeping, shared planning and ongoing communication are particularly important (see p64). For example:

▶ a diary can be used for handovers if necessary and a checklist as a work guide; job- sharers can communicate by telephone at the cross over point or the Wednesday evening;

▶ it may be necessary to have an hour's handover time; if the employees are willing to do this for no extra pay, the employer cannot argue that it would be too expensive;

▶ it may be easier, in some jobs, if the job-sharers do alternate days so that they are never away for more than one day at a time; in other jobs it may be possible to work for half of each day, though this is only likely to be viable if the job is local to the employee's home and/or school or nursery,

▶ in some jobs, it may be possible to split tasks and meetings; thus, one manager could take primary managerial responsibility for half the staff;

▶ it may be necessary to agree to some flexibility in relation to hours, for example both managers may need to be at the same meeting;

▶ the more senior the job, the more flexible the employee will need to be.

Remember

What is essential is a commitment from line managers to job-sharing because they are usually responsible for setting up the practical details.[2] Employers should remember the business advantages (see Chapter 8).

6 Employers should never make assumptions about what a woman wants to do on her return from maternity leave

Many women want to return part-time from maternity leave; some don't. Some employers make comments like, 'you won't want such a responsible job' or 'you will only want part-time work on your return'. Such remarks, which are not based on any discussions with the woman concerned, are likely to be discriminatory and, if acted on, give rise to a claim for compensation for unlawful discrimination.

7 Employers should apply the same rules for women and men

Some employers assume that it is only women who want shorter hours, part-time work and other child-friendly hours.

Surveys have found that child-friendly working practices are available to fathers to a far lesser degree than they are to mothers.[3] Failure to offer such hours to a man with primary responsibility for children when they are offered to a woman may be direct discrimination (see p26).

8 Employers should discuss with the woman what she wants to do

If a woman says she wants to return to the same job full-time after maternity leave, she is entitled to do so. If she says she wants to consider a change in hours, it is generally better to discuss how this can be achieved and plan for it at an early stage. It may mean that arrangements for maternity leave cover are planned differently. The employer should consider all the options which will fit in with the woman's childcare and with the job in question (see p84). This will involve open discussions with the woman about:

▶ the potential problems and how to resolve them (for example continuity, communication, consistency of decision making in management jobs),

▶ any flexibility the woman can offer to deal with problems (such as being contactable by telephone to deal with emergencies),

▶ whether the change in hours is sought on a temporary or permanent basis,

▶ whether the woman would be prepared to work full-time for a short period, pending the appointment of a job-share, and, if not, whether the hours can be covered by another employee (permanent or temporary),

▶ how to appoint a job-share and ensure that the arrangement works,

▶ if the agreement is for some working from home, what equipment is needed. Neither the employer nor the employee should assume that the employee will be working with a baby on her knee. If there is concern about this, the employer may want to ensure that there is suitable work space and time for the work to be done without interruption;

▶ any other concerns.

Remember
The advantages for the employer of retaining qualified staff and the extra productivity, commitment and improved morale which will result if the employee can be accommodated (see p87);

The offer of an inferior job on part-time hours or the same job but on a freelance basis is not equivalent and may lead to a claim of discrimination.

9 Employers should avoid having a policy of not allowing child-friendly hours

A blanket policy is likely to be challengeable as it means that no consideration has been given to the individual's circumstances (see p61).

10 Employers should adopt an equal opportunities policy and maternity policy

In *Todd*,[4] where the applicant won her claim for indirect sex discrimination after not being allowed to return to work part-time, the tribunal said 'We have in this decision laid strong emphasis on the need for this Council to adopt an equal opportunities policy'. Such a policy should include guidance on job-sharing and other child-friendly working practices, the procedure for making a request, how it will be dealt with, advertising jobs and practical details like the division of responsibilities, pay and benefits.

Some organisations with a policy on job-sharing, for example, Shell, Barclays, Gloucestershire County Council and Kingston and District Community Unit, allow all employees to apply for job-sharing and then consider whether the position can be job-shared. Other employers allow job-sharing of all jobs unless there is a good reason for exempting them. Some employers allow all their employees above a certain level to apply for job-sharing, while in others only staff below managerial grades can apply to job-share. The Family Planning Association, for example, has a clause in the contract which states 'all FPA employees have the right to return to their job on a part-time (not normally less than 16 hours per week) or job-share basis unless there is an exceptional reason why their job cannot be done as a part-time or job-share basis.'[5]

11 Employers should consider a job-share register

Some organisations have a job-share register where employees can register their interest in job-sharing and find out if an employee with a similar job might be able to job-share. This is a useful way of matching employees with similar needs. It also enables employers to discuss how a particular job could be job-shared including any practical problems and how they could be overcome.

12 Remember that conflict at work can lead to stress-related illness

It is very important that the employer responds quickly and sympathetically to a request to work child-friendly hours. It should never be dismissed without serious consideration and there should be discussion about how agreement could be achieved (see p101).

Occasionally a woman whose request to change her hours is not considered promptly or properly and who therefore fears she will lose her job, suffers stress-related illness. In *Gisborn*,[6] the tribunal found that a woman who was threatened with redundancy unless she returned full-time, suffered concentration problems, sleeplessness, stomach problems and nervous debility. She was awarded £1,500 in respect of the illness which the tribunal found was 'the direct consequence of the respondent's discriminatory act'. The compensation can be much higher and may include aggravated damages (see p165), particularly if evidence is given from a doctor about the effect on the woman. Employers should also be aware of their health and safety duties to employees; stress related illness may give rise to a claim for compensation for breach of the employer's duty of care under both statutory and common law.

13 The offer of part-time work as self-employed is not a suitable alternative

Some employers will agree to a woman working part-time but only if she becomes self-employed and loses the benefits of being an employee, for example, holidays, sick pay, and pension rights. However, tribunals are increasingly wary of employers trying to avoid their obligations to employees by making them self-employed and may find that the woman is in fact an employee, in which case she is entitled to continuity of service and all the benefits received by employees (see also p67).

In addition, if the job can be done part-time by a self-employed person, why can it not be done by a part-time employee?

Some women may prefer to be self-employed, but should take into account the loss of benefits and security associated with self-employment.

Remember

Working hours which are incompatible with childcare responsibilities, may be discriminatory and may be challenged whether they are existing requirements or newly imposed on the woman's return to work. These include long hours and overtime (particularly at short notice), inflexible hours, variable hours contracts, anti-social hours, mobility requirements.

14 Offer of four day week when only three is possible

An employer may offer a woman, who wants to work three days, a four day week instead. A woman wanting to challenge this will have to show that a considerably smaller proportion of women than men can comply with the requirement to work a four day week (not full-time). This may be difficult if the statistical evidence is not available in the workplace and/or in the labour force figures. However the information should be requested in the questionnaire and, in relation to the labour force, from the EOC.

Footnotes

[1] *Deacon v Leicestershire Constabulary* Case No. 65899/95.

[2] *Job-Sharing*, IDS (1994).

[3] *Family-friendly working arrangements in Britain*, Forth *et al*, Department for Education and Employment (1996).

[4] *Todd v Rushcliffe Borough Council* 11339/90 Nottingham IT 1.2.91.

[5] *Women Today*, MSF (1997).

[6] *Gisborn v Alliance and Leicester Building Society* 11925/94 Leicester IT 19.8.94.

Chapter 10

What if the employer refuses child-friendly hours?

The same principles apply whether an employer refuses child-friendly hours when requested or requires a woman to change to child-unfriendly hours.

1 When is negotiation at an end?

The time to give up negotiations and to decide whether to bring legal proceedings will depend on the circumstances:

▶ If the employer has said that there is no possibility of changing the hours, and it is 'full-time or nothing', there is little point in further negotiations;

▶ If the woman is told that 'it is very unlikely' but further consideration will be given to it, then she should wait until she receives a firm reply;

▶ If the employer does not make a decision for a considerable period, the woman should continue to press for a reply. There may then come a time when she should write to the employer giving a deadline for a reply. If there is still no reply, she will need to decide whether to resign (see p108);

▶ If, before the woman starts her maternity leave, the employer refuses to consider the request for different hours, she can make a further request on her return or prior to returning. However, she must watch for time limits (see p144ff).

2 The options on refusal

The options are:

a   to return to work in the same job on the same hours, perhaps under protest;

b   to accept less favourable terms or job in order to work the requested hours;

c   to resign and claim discrimination and constructive dismissal.

Remember

Always give the right notice of maternity leave and intention to return (see p128ff).

a   Returning to work on the same hours

If the woman feels that it will be impossible to do the same hours in the long term, but she cannot afford to resign, she should return on the same hours **provided** she makes it clear that she is doing so under protest. She can then make a claim to a tribunal while still working. However, bringing a claim against an employer is likely to make the working environment very stressful and may make it impossible for the woman to stay in the long term. It may be easier in a large organisation where there is a **policy** against part-time working over which the woman's immediate managers have no control and so do not feel personally involved. Where possible the woman should:

▶   ask the union, if there is one, to do the negotiation and representation;

▶   try to continue working as normal;

▶   ask for an early tribunal hearing date;

▶   avoid confrontational correspondence between the parties.

In order to avoid the possibility of the employer saying that a woman can work full-time, because she is doing so, it may be advisable to try and get the employer's agreement to taking holiday to shorten the week (see p52). If the stress is causing her ill-health she may have to see a doctor and take sick leave, though this should not be done lightly.

Remember

If a woman is forced to change her hours on return from maternity leave or otherwise, this may also be discriminatory and in breach of contract (see *Edwards* p41 and p123).

b   Accepting less favourable terms or job

The offer of self-employment

Some employers respond to a woman's request to work part-time by offering her self-employed status with an hourly rate of pay, no paid holidays or sick pay, no benefits, such as a pension, and no job security. This saves the employer significant costs. A woman, who cannot afford to be without work, may feel forced into accepting this.

Calling a woman 'self-employed' is not, however, conclusive and she may, in reality, be an employee, but there is a danger that:

▶   if she really is self-employed, she will lose her continuity of service and employment protection; note, however, that the self-employed are protected by the SDA (see p118);
▶   the woman will not be guaranteed work.

If a woman can show she is an employee (and this will be easier to do if her work situation is similar to when she was called an employee) she can claim protection from unfair dismissal, as well as discrimination, if she is no longer given any work.

Less favourable job

If a woman accepts a less favourable or temporary job in order to do different hours, she will not have a claim for either discrimination or unfair dismissal unless she accepts the job 'under protest' and brings proceedings without delay (see p139).

If a woman is offered an alternative job, on child-friendly hours, which the employer says is suitable, the woman may accept only to find that once in post, the job is not really suitable. As soon as she is aware that it is not suitable, she should write to the employer making it clear why it is not suitable and stating that she is doing it under protest. If there is another suitable post, she should ask to be considered for it. If not, she will then need to decide whether to resign and claim constructive dismissal. If so, there should not be too long a delay because there is a danger that the tribunal will say that she accepted the job (see p138).

Trial period with unsuitable hours

Where the employer imposes different hours on a woman's return from maternity leave or offers hours which are unsuitable, she needs to think about whether to try them out. If she does, she should make it clear that it is a trial period. However, if she knows they will be unsuitable, and there is no scope for negotiating, they is little point in a trial. In *Edwards*,[1] where a new roster was imposed, the tribunal said that an employee faced with a choice between working a new roster and, if it did not prove satisfactory, having to leave or be dismissed for breach of contract, and the alternative of an enhanced voluntary severance package, could reasonably not risk working the roster when she was quite clear in her own mind that she would not be able to do so for very long.

c   Resignation

A woman who resigns will have suffered sex discrimination and may also be able to claim constructive unfair dismissal (see p138).

The woman should first be quite clear that she cannot continue working. The decision to resign should not be taken in order to strengthen a discrimination or unfair dismissal claim – though if the woman has decided to resign, she should do so without too much delay (see p139). The woman should consider the consequences including:

▶   the financial implications; apart from the loss of income from earnings, there may be other lost benefits, such as pension, company car, etc; if the woman has any debts she needs to consider how these can be paid;

▶   the fact that it is often more difficult to get another job when unemployed;

▶   the stress involved in being unemployed set against the stress of continuing to work long hours;

▶   whether there is any further scope for negotiation about different hours.

When to resign

A woman should not resign until the employer has refused the woman a change in hours. Where the employer has said that s/he will be imposing new unsuitable hours in the future, it may be premature to resign until the hours are actually imposed; the possibility of a change in hours will not usually be enough to justify resignation and a claim of constructive dismissal (see p32).

Once the woman has decided she will resign if she is not allowed to change her hours, important considerations about when to resign are:

i **Have all attempts to negotiate failed?** It is not advisable to resign at a time when the employer has said s/he will reconsider a woman's request. All options should be considered (see pp84 and 101). Negotiations about child-friendly hours may be short and end with the employer either agreeing or refusing. Alternatively, they may take place over a period of time. It is important to continue negotiating if there is **any** possibility that this may resolve matters.

ii **If the employer has refused any change in working hours**, the woman should write to her/him stating that: it is not possible to continue on the same hours; asking for the decision to be reversed within seven days; and stating that, if it is not, in view of the breakdown of trust and confidence and the discrimination, she will have no alternative but to resign and claim constructive dismissal (see p206 for precedent).

iii **If there is no satisfactory response within the seven days**, a further letter should be written by the employee stating that in view of the employer's refusal there has been discrimination and a breakdown of the relationship of trust and confidence and she is resigning and will be claiming discrimination and constructive dismissal (see p204).

iv **If the employer fails to reply at all to a request for a change in hours** the employee should not be expected to wait indefinitely. The employee should write a final letter to the employer saying that if there is no response within a specified period (eg seven days) she will assume that her request has been refused and resign).

v **If the employer says it depends on finding another employee**, to work the remaining hours (see p98), this is a more difficult situation. It may take some time to recruit a new employee yet the woman may find it impossible to continue working the same hours. If the woman resigns before the employer has found a replacement, there is a danger that the tribunal will say that the refusal to allow reduced hours in the short term is justifiable, particularly as the employer is attempting to find a long term solution. The question as to whether the employer should allow the woman to reduce her hours in the short term, pending recruitment, will depend on the circumstances, such as her immediate needs and the needs of the business (see Chapter 6).

vi If the woman is asked to stay at home meanwhile, and does not want to do so, she will need to consider the options (see p98) If she is treated less favourably, because of making the request and alleging that refusal would be discriminatory, this may be victimisation (see p115).

vii If the contract is not continuing: if the woman wants to resign during her maternity absence, there can be no dismissal (or constructive dismissal) if there is no contract (see p135ff). She should first give 21 days notice of her intention to return which will revive the contract (see pp129 and 136). This may change in 1999 when new legislation is likely to provide that the contract does continue during maternity absence.

viii Working out the notice period: most contracts provide that an employee must give a minimum period of notice. In most circumstances a woman should give notice, though the employer may well waive the notice so that she can leave immediately. If the woman feels physically unwell with stress, she should consider getting advice from her doctor.

3 When to mention the law

Persuasion is better than confrontation. Pointing out that a refusal to allow a woman to do child-friendly working hours may be discriminatory may have a different effect depending on the attitude of the employer. Some will see it as confrontational and it will strengthen their resistance; some may take legal advice and yet others may be more inclined to listen and negotiate, fearing a claim for discrimination. Showing the employer the Maternity Alliance leaflet called 'Child-friendly working hours: your rights' may help to persuade the employer of the benefits of allowing a change in hours and the dangers of not doing so, without undermining the employment relationship.

4 Settlement

It is quite common for the employer to offer the woman some money to fend off proceedings. If this happens, it is important to try and get some legal advice about an appropriate settlement (see p159).

If there is a lawyer or adviser involved, it may be better to let them do the negotiations, although it will depend on who is likely to negotiate a better deal!

5 When should an adviser or lawyer become involved?

A woman may seek advice from an advice agency or solicitor about her right to change her hours or work from home. Whether an adviser or lawyer gets involved in negotiations depends on the situation. It may produce the desired outcome or it may antagonise the employer and lead to deteriorating relations with the employee.

The adviser can, however, play an important role in advising the woman how to negotiate with her employer and what steps to take to protect her rights.

6 When to bring legal proceedings

When deciding whether to issue legal proceedings, it is important to consider:

▶ first and foremost, time limits; remember these are short; proceedings must be issued within three months (less one day) of the act of discrimination (see p144ff);

▶ the added stress of issuing proceedings whilst still an employee;

▶ whether it may make it more difficult to find another job; this may happen if the work which the woman does is very specialised and other employers are likely to find out about the proceedings; note, however, that there is protection from victimisation (see p115);

▶ whether the employee's partner works for the same employer; occasionally the woman's partner works for the same organisation. If this is the case, and there is concern that he may be treated less favourably as a result, this may influence the decision about taking proceedings. This is very much a personal decision and will depend on the family's income, the likelihood of either party finding alternative work etc.

▶ the potential cost if a solicitor is involved (but check legal costs insurance). See Chapter 17 for how to get advice and assistance.

Remember

A woman wanting to return on child-friendly working hours has the right to return to the same, or equivalent, job; she should not have to accept an inferior job in order to work child- friendly hours.

7 Using the questionnaire

Once negotiations have broken down, it is very important to get as much information as possible, as early as possible, about the reasons for the employer's objections so the woman can gather all the necessary information to counter these objections. This can be obtained through the questionnaire (see p143).

Practical tips

- ▶ make a note of all conversations and meetings after they happen; do not throw away the original note, even if it is subsequently typed up;
- ▶ keep copies of all relevant documents;
- ▶ find out information from other employees;
- ▶ confirm in writing any requests for child-friendly arrangements, making clear what hours would be possible;
- ▶ always watch out for time limits;
- ▶ always give the correct notices within the time limits.

Remember

The employer cannot usually impose different hours. Many women want to return to work from maternity leave on the **same** hours, either because they do not want to work reduced hours or cannot afford the loss of income. Employers who assume that a woman will only want to return part-time and change her job duties accordingly will also be discriminating. A woman is entitled to return to the same job on the same hours if that is what she wants to do (see Chapter 13).

Footnote

[1] *London Underground v Edwards* [1988] IRLR 364, CA.

Chapter 11

Relevant provisions of the Sex Discrimination Act 1975

A claim for discrimination is made under the SDA(see Appendix 1). A woman must:

▶ show there has been sex discrimination and

▶ she is protected by the SDA (for example, she is an employee and not within one of the exclusions) and

▶ the employer has done a prohibited act.

1 Different types of discrimination

a   Direct sex discrimination

Direct discrimination occurs where a woman is or would be treated less favourably than a man and the reason for the less favourable treatment is because she is a woman. Thus, denial of a job or promotion to a woman because she is a woman will be direct discrimination. The question is whether, '**but for**' the fact that she is a woman, would she have been appointed or promoted? If the answer is 'yes', it will be direct discrimination.[1]

Any less favourable treatment of a woman because she is pregnant or has recently given birth or taken maternity leave will also be direct sex discrimination. There is no need to prove that the woman has been treated less favourably than a man in a similar situation. In *Webb*,[2] the House of Lords held that less favourable treatment of a woman because she is pregnant or has recently given birth was unlawful discrimination in itself.

Examples

▶ where a woman is not allowed to take time off when a man would be allowed time off;

▶ where a man is not allowed to work flexible hours in order to take his children to school when a woman would be allowed to do so. Such a claim by a man may also be possible where a woman is bringing a claim for indirect sex discrimination because she is not allowed to work reduced hours. A man could claim that, if the woman won, it would be discrimination not to allow him to reduce his hours. In **Preston**,[3] part-time women were claiming pro rata pension entitlement with full-time employees. Part-time men also made a claim on the basis that, if the women won, they too should be entitled to pro rata pension; if their claims were not allowed they would be prejudiced if their compensation could only be backdated for two years. The men's claim was allowed to proceed.

The EAT has held that refusal to allow a woman to return to work part-time is not direct discrimination.[4] It would only be direct discrimination if a man in a similar job was allowed to work part-time.

b   Indirect sex discrimination

Indirect discrimination is concerned with practices which have the effect of discriminating against women and which cannot be justified by the needs of the job. Such practices are usually connected to the fact that, in practice, women still have primary responsibility for children (see Chapters 1 and 4).

c   Direct and indirect marital discrimination

It is not only sex discrimination which is unlawful but also marital discrimination. Refusal to appoint or promote a woman (or man) because s/he is married will be direct marital discrimination.

A requirement to work full-time or long hours may be indirect marital discrimination. The requirement is likely to disadvantage a substantially higher proportion of married women because they are more likely to have children than single women.

It may also be possible to argue that refusal to allow a married man to work child-friendly hours affects married men particularly harshly compared to single men. It may be difficult to prove this because few men, whether married or not, do in fact take main responsibility for children. If there was evidence that a smaller proportion of married than single men could comply with a requirement to work, say, full-time, a married man could claim indirect marital discrimination.

d Victimisation

It is unlawful to treat a woman less favourably because she has either:

▶ brought a complaint under the SDA, ie issued proceedings, or

▶ given evidence or information in connection with proceedings (such as supporting a claim), or

▶ done anything else under or by reference to the SDA; this is very wide, or

▶ made allegations against the employer that it has acted unlawfully under the Act (such as stating that it is discriminatory not to allow the woman to work part-time).[5]

If a woman asks to work part-time, complains of discrimination, and, as a result, is denied the opportunity to do particular work, or refused promotion or otherwise treated less favourably, this will be victimisation.

Remember the Equal Opportunities Code of Practice

The Equal Opportunities Commission (EOC) has produced a code of practice, the purpose of which is to eliminate discrimination in employment and to promote equality of opportunity.[6] The code provides guidance for employers about practices which they recommend should be adopted to promote equality. The code does not have the same effect as legislation but failure by an employer to observe any provision of a code may be taken into account by a tribunal or court.[7] A tribunal must take the code into account and failure to do so may result in a successful appeal (see p24ff).[8]

The EOC Code recommends that employers should consider whether certain jobs can be carried out on a part-time or flexi-time basis (see para 43).

Remember

The EC Recommendation on Childcare and the guidance on its implementation (see Appendix 2).

2 Which workers are protected?

The following can make a claim of discrimination:

▶ job applicants,[9]
▶ employees,[10]
▶ the self-employed.[11] However, the ERA only protects and provides rights for employees, not the self-employed. Thus, only employees are entitled to redundancy pay, protection from ordinary unfair dismissal, maternity rights. The question as to whether a person is employed or self-employed will depend on a number of factors.[12]
▶ partners,[13]
▶ contract workers, ie individuals working for a person, called the principal, who are not employed by the principal but by a third party such as an employment agency. Contract workers include, for example, temporary secretaries who are employed by the agency but sent to work for different companies. The secretary may be an employee of the agency, so is protected as an employee. She will also be protected from discrimination by her principal – ie the person for whom she does the work,[14]
▶ barristers and advocates.[15]

3 Prohibited acts of discrimination

Discrimination alone is not unlawful. What is prohibited is discrimination, direct or indirect, in relation to certain areas of employment:

a   the arrangements made by an employer for deciding who should be offered employment, for example, selection procedures;
b   the terms and conditions on which a person is offered a job;
c   not employing a woman, for example, because she is pregnant, might become pregnant or because she has asked to work reduced hours; the latter may be indirect discrimination;

d   opportunities for transfer, training or promotion;
e   benefits, facilities or services;
f   dismissal, for example, where a woman resigns because the employer will not allow her to work child-friendly hours;
g   any other detriment. This means treating a woman less favourably in any other way. It includes not allowing a woman to work child-friendly hours.[16]

Partners are protected in respect of recruitment and the terms of partnership offered, access to benefits, facilities or services, expulsion or being subject to any other detriment.

Contract workers are protected in relation to the terms on which she is allowed to work, not allowing her to continue to work, in access to benefits, facilities or services and by subjecting her to any other detriment.

Examples

The following could make a claim of indirect sex discrimination:

▶   a job applicant who is not considered for a job because she wants to do it part-time;

▶   an employee who is not allowed to return to work part-time after maternity leave;

▶   a self-employed person who is not considered for work because she only works part-time;

▶   a contract worker who is told she will not be allocated to a business because they require her to work overtime; she will have a claim against the principal. If the agency who employs her terminates her employment because she will not work overtime, she may also have a claim against the agency;

▶   an employed solicitor who is told that if she works part-time she will never be made a partner.

4 Discrimination by bodies other than employers

In addition, it is unlawful for the following bodies to discriminate:

a   **an employment agency** must not discriminate in the terms on which it offers its services, or by refusing to provide its services, or in the way it provides its services. If an agency refused to provide services to a woman because she only wanted part-time work, this may be indirectly discriminatory;[17]

b   **trades unions and professional and employers' organisations** must not discriminate in relation to access to membership nor against members. Refusal to allow a person to join because they work part-time may be discriminatory;[18]

c   **training bodies must not discriminate.** Limiting training to those who can attend residential courses or evening sessions may be indirectly discriminatory if not justified. It is a requirement which is likely to have an adverse effect on women with childcare responsibilities.[19]

5 Exclusions from the SDA

There are some exceptions under the SDA but these are unlikely to be relevant to the type of claims covered in this book. They include, for example, the provision of special treatment for women relating to pregnancy, childbirth and maternity leave; this means that men are not entitled to the same protection as pregnant women or women on maternity leave, so cannot bring a discrimination claim because they are not entitled to paternity leave.[20]

Remember
The SDA applies to Crown employees, the police, and prison officers, although there are some exceptions, such as height requirements, for the police and prison officers.[21] It also applies to the armed forces except for requirements necessary to ensure 'combat effectiveness'.[22]

6 Unfair dismissal

A woman may have a claim for discriminatory dismissal under the SDA and for unfair dismissal under the ERA. A discriminatory dismissal will generally also be an unfair one, giving rise to a claim for compensation under the ERA.[23] Where there has been a breach of the terms of the woman's contract by the employer, this may entitle the woman to resign and claim constructive dismissal (see Chapter 14 for unfair dismissal provisions).

Footnotes

[1] *James v Eastleigh BC* [1990] IRLR 288.
[2] *Webb v EMO Air Cargo (UK) Ltd* (No 2) [1995] IRLR 645 HL.
[3] *Preston and Others v (1) Wolverhampton Healthcare NHS Trust (2) Secretary of State for Health* [1997] IRLR 233.
[4] *British Telecommunications plc v Roberts and Longstaffe* [1996] IRLR 601.
[5] SDA s4.
[6] SDA s56A.
[7] SDA s56A(10).
[8] *Berry v Bethlem and Maudsley NHS Trust* and *Hinks v Riva Systems* [1997] DCLD No 31, 1.
[9] SDA s6.
[10] SDA ss6 and 82.
[11] SDA ss6 and 82.
[12] *Employment Law: an advisers' handbook*, Kibling T and Lewis T, LAG, 3rd edn, (1996).
[13] SDA s11.
[14] SDA s9.
[15] The provisions for barristers are slightly different (SDA ss35A and 35B).
[16] SDA s6.
[17] SDA s15.
[18] SDA s12.
[19] SDA s14.
[20] SDA s2(2).
[21] SDA s17, 18 and 85.
[22] SDA s85(4); Sex Discrimination Act 1975 (Application to Armed Forces etc) Regulations 1994 SI No 3276.
[23] *Clarke v Eley (IMI) Kynoch Ltd* [1982] IRLR 482.

Chapter 12

Relevant European law

A claim for indirect sex discrimination can be brought without relying on EC law and, in the majority of cases, it is not mentioned. However, it is often useful to be aware of EC law's provisions and their effect in the UK. In particular, the EC Recommendation and Guidance on Childcare is very useful. (See Appendix 2)

1 What use is EC law?

EC law may seem an added complication. In fact, it is much simpler and easier to understand than the parallel UK law. The main provisions of EC law are summarised in the box.

European law, like UK law, prohibits direct and indirect discrimination in employment.

2 Effect of EC law

Wherever possible, UK courts and tribunals must interpret UK law in line with EC law.[1] If there is any ambiguity in UK law it must be resolved so as to be in line with EC law.[2] If this is not possible, because there is a clear conflict, then in some situations, where either the employer is a public body or the applicant is relying on Article 119 of the Treaty of Rome, EC law overrides UK law (see p123). This includes cases where the employer is an 'emanation' of the state, ie providing a public service, which is under the control of the state and where that body has special powers beyond those which result from the normal rules which apply in relations between individuals. This would include public authorities such as local authorities or health authorities.[3]

EC Provision	What it says	How it can be used
Equal Treatment Directive [4]	There shall be no discrimination whatsoever on grounds of sex either directly or indirectly by reference in particular to marital or family status	Aid to interpretation in all cases; mainly implemented by SDA. Binding on public bodies (emanations of the State)
European Council Recommendation on Childcare	Recommends initiatives which create a workplace which takes account of the needs of all working parents	Persuasive, but not binding (see p126)
Guidance on implementing the Council Childcare Recommendation	Identifies measures to assist parents, eg reduced hours, job-sharing, flexitime	Guidance only (see Appendix 2)
Article 119 of the Treaty of Rome	Provides for equal pay for equal work, including pro rata rights for part-time workers	Binding on UK courts; only relevant to equal pay (Chapter 7)
Equal Pay Directive	Explains Article 119	As it does not add to Art 119, its effect is primarily interpretative

3 Relevant provisions

a Article 119 of the Treaty of Rome

This provides that men and women should receive the same pay and benefits for equal work. Many of the decisions of the European Court of Justice have held that part-time workers, where these are predominantly women, should receive the same pro rata rights and benefits as full-time workers, unless the difference can be justified by the employer (see chapter 7).

Pay and benefits are defined very widely under Article 119 to include any consideration, whether in cash or in kind, which the worker receives, directly or indirectly, in respect of his employment from his employer. The key is whether the benefit is received because of the employment relationship.[5] It includes pay supplements, shift premia, merit and performance pay, pensions, redundancy payments, sick pay, maternity pay, and travel concessions.[6]

Article 119 is effectively part of UK law. Even where there is a conflict between UK and EC law, tribunals and courts must follow Article 119 and not the conflicting UK provisions.

b   The Equal Pay Directive

This provides that all discrimination on the ground of sex in respect of all aspects of pay must be eliminated. It explains the effect of Article 119 but does not add further rights.

c   The Equal Treatment Directive (ETD)

The ETD states that:

> 'there shall be no discrimination whatsoever on grounds of sex either directly or indirectly by reference in particular to marital or family status'.

It prohibits discrimination in:
- access to employment,
- access to training and vocational guidance,
- working conditions,
- promotion,
- dismissal.

In *Edwards*,[7] an indirect sex discrimination case about working hours (see below) the EAT echoed what the CA had said, in *Seymour Smith*,[8] about the purpose of the Directive, that it is:

> 'to eliminate all sex discrimination in the employment field. Equality of treatment is the paramount consideration'.

The Directives are only binding where the employer is a public body, or more accurately described as an 'emanation of the State'. Thus local authorities, health authorities, and Government departments are all public bodies. The Directives take precedence where the employer is such a body.

d The European Council Recommendation on Childcare

Although the recommendation is not legally binding, it is a statement of policy which may be taken into account by tribunals as an 'aid to interpretation'. The ECJ has ruled that domestic courts are bound to take recommendations into account in order to decide disputes.[10]

The Recommendation suggests that initiatives be taken to create a workplace which takes into account the needs of all working parents. The Recommendation recommends four areas for action:

i   the provision of childcare services while parents are working, training or seeking a job;
ii   special leave for employed parents with responsibility for the care and upbringing of children;
iii initiatives so that the workplace takes into account the needs of all working parents with responsibility for the care of children;
iv   the sharing of occupations, family and upbringing responsibilities arising from the care of children between women and men.

The Guidance on Implementing the 1992 Council Recommendation on Childcare identified measures that can be taken to assist parents in the reconciliation of their work and family roles.[11]

The Recommendation will be relevant where a woman with childcare responsibilities is not allowed to work part-time or flexible hours or where a part-time worker is treated less favourably than a full-time worker (see Chapter 7). See Appendix 2 for extracts.

e The Working Time Regulations

The Regulations[12] lay down minimum health and safety requirements relating to working hours. The main provisions are for:

▶   a minimum period of paid annual leave (3 weeks increasing to 4 in 1999);

- ▶ a maximum normal working period of eight hours in 24 for night workers;
- ▶ a maximum average working week of 48 hours calculated over a period of up to 17 weeks.
- ▶ a break of not less than 20 minutes after a maximum of six hours.

Thus, if a woman is required to work more than 48 hours per week over a 17-week period this will be a breach of the Regulations as well as, arguably, indirect discrimination. There are some exceptions to the Regulations. The details are outside the scope of this book.

f   The Parental Leave Directive

The Government have said they will adopt the provisions of this Directive,[13] but it is unlikely to be in force before the end of 1999. Apart from three months parental leave for both parents, the Directive provides that workers must be entitled to time off work for urgent family reasons where sickness or accident make the immediate presence of the worker indispensable.

g   The Burden of Proof Directive

The aim of the Burden of Proof Directive[14] is to make the 'principle of equal treatment' more effective and to enable those who have been discriminated against to get an effective remedy. Where an applicant can, from the facts, show a presumption that there may have been discrimination, the onus will be on the employer to show there was no discrimination. It also provides a new definition of indirect discrimination. This Directive must be in force by 1 January 2001.

The Burden of Proof Directive is a useful starting point for an EC definition of indirect discrimination:

> 'Indirect discrimination shall exist where an apparently neutral provision, criterion or practice disadvantages a substantially higher proportion of the members of one sex unless that provision, criterion or practice is appropriate and necessary and can be justified by objective factors unrelated to sex.'

This reflects European caselaw, and in particular, ECJ decisions such as *Bilka*,[15] where the ECJ held that the exclusion of part-time employees from a pension scheme would be unlawful

> *'where that exclusion affects a far greater number of women than men, unless the undertaking shows that the exclusion is based on objectively justified factors unrelated to any discrimination on grounds of sex'.*

h The Part-time Work Directive

When this comes into force in April 2000, it will provide for:
▶ equal rights for part-time workers – men and women;
▶ Member States to facilitate access to part-time work for men and women in order to reconcile professional and family life;
▶ employers to give consideration to measures to facilitate access to part-time work at all levels of the enterprise, including skilled and managerial positions.[16]

The Directive, when implemented, will not provide a 'right' to work child friendly hours, although employers must consider requests to transfer to part-time work – and back again – at all levels of the enterprise.

Footnotes

1 *Marleasing SA v La Comercial Internacional de Alimentacion SA* [1990] ECR 1-4135, followed by the HL in *Litster v Forth Dry Dock Co Ltd* [1989] IRLR 161, HL.
2 *Garland v British Railway Engineering Ltd* [1982] 2 All ER 402, HL.
3 *Foster and Others v British Gas plc* [1990] IRLR 353.
4 The Equal Treatment Directive does not take UK law much further except that some of the technical problems with the definition of indirect discrimination may not apply under the ETD.
5 *EC Commission v Belgium* [1993] IRLR 404.
6 *Discrimination at Work*, Palmer C, et al LAG (1997).
7 *London Underground v Edwards* (No 2) [1997] IRLR 157.
8 *R v Secretary of State for Employment ex p Seymour Smith* [1995] IRLR 464, CA.
9 92/241/EEC.
10 *Grimaldi v Fonds des Maladies Professionelles* [1990] IRLR 400, ECJ.
11 Guidance on Implementing the Council Recommendation on Childcare, 92/241/EEC.
12 *The Working Time Regulations* 1998 si 1998/1833 implemented by the EC. Thy came into force on 1st October 1998. *Working Time Directive* 93/104/EEC.
13 *Parental Leave Directive* 96/34/EC.
14 *Draft Directive on Burden of Proof* 97/C302/02, EOR 76 Nov/Dec 1997.
15 *Bilka-Kaufhaus GmbH v Weber von Hartz* Case 170/84 [1986] IRLR 317.
16 *Part-time Workers Directive* 98/23/EC, due to be in force by April 2000.

Chapter 13

Maternity rights

A woman claiming indirect sex and/or marital discrimination, where the employer will not allow her to return to work from maternity leave or absence on child friendly working hours, must first:

► comply with the necessary notice provisions in order to be entitled to get the benefits of maternity leave and absence – either statutory or contractual (see p129ff);

► show she still has a contract of employment if she intends to resign and claim discrimination and constructive dismissal (see p135);

► have tried to negotiate child-friendly hours and been refused or received no response from her employer (see Chapter 8);

► bring proceedings in the tribunal **within** three months of the discrimination (see p144).

Remember

There are rights to paid time off for antenatal care and protection from health and safety risks but these are outside the scope of this guide (except see p50 for relevance of health and safety provisions to breast-feeding).

1 Maternity leave

All employees are entitled to 14 weeks maternity leave, irrespective of their length of service, hours of work, pay and whether they are temporary or permanent employees. Under the provisions of the Fairness at Work White Paper this will increase to eighteen weeks. The only conditions are that:

- ► the woman must be employed at the 11th week before the expected week of childbirth and
- ► she gives the right notice.

a Notice for general maternity leave

The woman must give her employer written notice, at least 21 days before her maternity leave starts, or, if that is not reasonably practicable, as soon as it is reasonably practicable of:

a the fact that she is pregnant; and
b the expected week of childbirth (EWC); or the date of the birth if it has occurred;
c the fact that she wishes to be paid statutory maternity pay; and
d if she is entitled to extended maternity absence, that she intends to return to work.

In addition, the woman must inform her employer, in writing if s/he requests it, at least 21 days before her maternity leave starts, or, if that is not reasonably practicable, as soon as is reasonably practicable of the date she intends to start her leave.[1] However, this 21 day time limit does not apply in either of the above cases if:

- ► the woman is absent because of her pregnancy in the six weeks before the EWC and her employer insists she start her leave; or
- ► she gives birth before she has notified her employer; or
- ► she gives birth before the notice expires.

Clearly, in these circumstances, it is impossible to give the required notice and the woman need only give notice, either of the birth or that her absence is due to pregnancy, as soon as possible.

b Requirement to provide doctor's certificate if requested

If the employer asks the woman to provide a doctor's or midwife's certificate giving the EWC, she must do so.[2] The request must clearly require a certificate and this will usually be a MAT B1. Failure to provide a certificate after being asked to do so, means that the woman may lose her right to statutory maternity leave and absence.[3]

c   Start of maternity leave

Usually, the woman can choose when her leave starts, though it cannot begin earlier than the 11th week before the EWC. This is the week the baby is due. It begins at midnight on the Saturday, so the first day is Sunday.[4] It will be the date she notified to the employer. The employer may insist on a woman's leave starting immediately if, during the six weeks before the EWC, she is absent **because of** her pregnancy.[5] This may be because she has a pregnancy-related sickness or gives birth early.

d   The contract continues during maternity leave

During the 14 week period the contract of employment, whether written or not, continues. The woman is entitled to all benefits under the contract except 'remuneration' – ie pay.

2 Extended maternity absence

A woman who has been employed continuously, by the same employer, for two years at the beginning of the 11th week before the expected week of childbirth is entitled to return to work up to 29 weeks after the beginning of the week in which the baby was born.[6] The two year requirement is likely to change to one year under the Fairness at Work proposals. The absence period begins immediately after the expiry of the 14 week leave.

a   Notice for extended maternity absence

There are two further notice provisions for extended maternity absence. As well as giving the notice set out above, the woman must:

i   give written notice to the employer, at least 21 days before the day on which she proposed to return, of her intention to return on that day.[7] Thus, notice must be given not later than 26 weeks after the actual week of childbirth. There is no provision for late notice to be given, unless the return is postponed, either because the woman is sick, in which case she can postpone her return by four weeks, or the employer postpones her return by up to four weeks;[8]

ii   where, not earlier than 21 days before the end of her 14 week maternity leave period, ie after 11 weeks of leave, the employer writes to
     the woman asking for written confirmation that she intends to
     return after the extended maternity absence, the employee must
     provide such written confirmation within 14 days of receiving the
     request, or if not reasonably practicable, as soon as is reasonably
     practicable. The employer's request must be in writing and must
     explain the effect of this provision, ie that the woman will lose her
     right to return if she does not reply in writing within 14 days. The
     woman is not obliged to give the actual date for her return until 21
     days before she is due to return.

b   Start of extended maternity absence

Extended maternity absence begins at the expiry of the 14 weeks maternity leave period.

c   The contractual position during extended maternity absence

During the extended maternity absence period, whether or not the contract of employment continues will depend on what the employer and
employee have agreed (see p136).

3 More favourable contractual rights

Some employers provide more generous maternity leave and pay than
the statutory provision.

It is important to check whether there is any agreement, written or
verbal, between the employer and employee and the terms of the agreement. Where there is a statutory and contractual right the woman can
take advantage of whichever right is, in any respect, more favourable.[9]

Remember
A woman who is negotiating a return to work on a shorter or flexible
hours arrangement must give the appropriate notice, including the fact
that she wants to return to the same job, even if:
▶   the employer is aware of the woman's intentions to return;

► it looks as if the woman will not be able to return because the employer will not allow her to return on different hours.

If the employer asks her to confirm that she will return full-time, she should reply by saying:

'I am writing to confirm that I will be returning to my job as ... on ... I confirm that I would like to return part-time/job-share/with reduced hours.' [It is possible to ask for any option in the alternative].

Note

If a woman gives notice to return to her job part-time, there is a danger the tribunal will find she has not given the proper notice. This happened in *McNamara*[10] where notice was given of an intention to return part-time to the same job. Arguably, this is wrong and too legalistic an approach but it is not worth risking.

She should give notice of her intention to return to the same job and then ask to return part-time. Failure to give notice may lead to the woman losing her rights. Although the contract may continue giving the woman protection from ordinary unfair dismissal (see Chapter 14), she should not rely on that.

4 Return to the same job

a   After 14 weeks Maternity Leave

A woman returning to work after maternity leave has a right to return to the same job with the same terms and conditions. The job must be exactly the same. The position is no different to any other absence, such as holiday or sickness.

Where a woman returns at the end of the 14 weeks she does not need to give any notice before returning. If she wants to return earlier, seven days notice must be given to the employer.

Dismissal or resignation during maternity leave

The contract of employment continues during the maternity leave period. If an employer refuses to allow a woman to return, this will be a dismissal (see p136).

If a woman resigns during maternity leave because, for example, she is not allowed to change her hours, she can claim discrimination (see p141).

b   Return after extended maternity absence

The right to return to work after extended maternity absence is slightly different. The right to return is:
- with the same employer, and
- in the job in which the woman was then employed,
- on no less favourable terms and conditions than she would have had she not been absent,
- otherwise on terms and conditions not less favourable than those which would have applied had she not been absent.[11]

If possible, the woman should be given the same job. If this is not possible the job must at least be:
- of the same type and nature, in the same capacity and in the same place, for example, secretary to a director reporting to the chief executive is unlikely to be the same as PA to the chief executive;
- on the same or equivalent terms and conditions as to pay; if there has been a pay rise while the woman was on maternity leave, she should receive this on her return.[12]

c   Two exceptions:

There are two exceptions to the right to return:

i   small employers
In order to rely on this, the employer must show:
- the number of employees is five or less; this includes employees for associated employers;
- it was not reasonably practicable for the employer to give the woman her original job back; and
- it was not reasonably practicable to offer the woman suitable alternative work, ie work which is suitable for her, appropriate and on equivalent terms and conditions.[13]

ii   offer of suitable alternative work
The employer must show:
- it is not reasonably practicable to allow the woman to return to the

same job; this does not include a redundancy situation;

▶ s/he has offered the woman suitable alternative work (see above) and the woman has either accepted it or unreasonably refused it.[14]

Note

The burden is on the employer to show one of the exceptions apply. Even if one of the exceptions apply, refusal to allow a woman her job back may still be discriminatory.

d   Failure to allow a woman to return on the same terms

Where an employer does not allow a woman to return to the same or equivalent job, as set out above, this will be a deemed dismissal because she has been denied her right to return.[15] The question is whether the dismissal is discriminatory, unfair, automatically unfair or all three (see Chapters 11 and 14).

e   Redundancy on maternity leave

A woman who is made redundant while on maternity leave or absence is entitled to be offered a suitable alternative vacancy. She should also consider whether the redundancy, and her selection, was connected to her pregnancy or maternity leave. If so, it will be automatically unfair and discriminatory (s99 ERA).

Footnotes

1   ERA s74(1).
2   ERA s75(2).
3   ERA s75(2).
4   ERA s235.
5   ERA s72(1)(b).
6   ERA s79.
7   ERA s82(1).
8   ERA s82.
9   ERA ss78 and 85.
10   *McNamara v Serical S.A.R.L.* Case No: 49257/92 Birmingham 18.11.93.
11   ERA s79.
12   ERA s235(1).
13   ERA s96(2).
14   ERA s96(3).
15   ERA s96(1).

Chapter 14

Unfair and constructive dismissal

The main claim, where a woman is refused child-friendly working hours, is for discrimination (see Chapter 2). However, she may also have a claim for unfair and/or discriminatory dismissal.

1 Dismissal – including constructive dismissal and redundancy

A dismissal may be unfair (see p137) and/or discriminatory. A discriminatory dismissal, contrary to S6(2) (b) of the SDA, will generally be unfair under the ERA.[1] Thus, if a woman is dismissed or resigns because she cannot work child-friendly hours, she should make a claim for:

▶ discrimination in that she has suffered a detriment (SDA); and/or
▶ discriminatory dismissal (SDA); and/or
▶ unfair dismissal (ERA).

There are three main questions to consider in an unfair dismissal claim:
a   Does the contract still exists?
b   Has there been a dismissal?
c   What is the reason for the dismissal?

a   Does the contract still exist?

Up until the end of the 14 weeks maternity leave period, the contract continues, unless it has been terminated by either the employer or employee.

The difficult question is whether the contract continues during extended maternity absence. This will depend on what the contract says, the agreement of the parties and the surrounding facts. The Court of Appeal is due to decide the question in late 1998 in *Halfpenny*.[2] Note, however, that there are proposals to amend the legislation so that the contract continues during extended maternity absence.[3]

If the contract does not exist during the absence, a claim for unfair dismissal and discrimination can then only be made if a woman has given her 21 days notice to return. Once she has given notice of her return, she will have exercised her right to return and will have revived her contract even if it did not exist during her absence. If she is sick on the day she is due to return, she should be treated like any other sick employee.[4] It is therefore advisable to give 21 days notice before resigning, otherwise there is a danger that it will not be a dismissal.

Contractual clause stating contract does not exist during absence

Even if there is a clause in the woman's contract stating that the contract does not continue during extended maternity absence, this may be overridden by the statute. In *Crees*,[5] the CA accepted that the statute overrides the contract. There can therefore be unfair dismissal even though the contract states that it comes to an end when the woman fails to return. In addition, such a provision in the contract may be discriminatory, if extended maternity absence is the only absence which automatically triggers the suspension of the contract. (But note that 21 days notice of return must always be given).

b   Has there been a dismissal?

A dismissal will occur where:

i   the employer terminates the employee's contract – with or without giving her notice; this includes, for example, dismissal for misconduct or redundancy;[6]

ii   a fixed term contract comes to an end and is not renewed on the same terms;[7]

iii the employer does not allow a woman to return to the same job after maternity leave,[8]

iv   the employer does not allow a woman to return to substantially the same job, on the same terms and conditions, after maternity absence;[9]

v   a woman resigns in response to the employer's breach of contract; this may be because the relationship of trust and confidence has broken down and/or the employer has discriminated against the woman.[10] This is constructive dismissal.

c What is the reason for the dismissal? Is it discriminatory and/or unfair?

i Ordinary unfair dismissal

Protection against ordinary unfair dismissal, unlike automatically unfair dismissal, only applies to women with two year's service. This may change to one year under the Fairness at Work proposals and in *Seymour Smith*,[11] the ECJ is due to decide whether the two year qualifying period is indirectly discriminatory. An employer may lawfully dismiss an employee for one of a number of 'fair' reasons including:

▶   capability (eg skill, aptitude, health);
▶   conduct (eg bad timekeeping, absenteeism, misconduct);
▶   redundancy (provided the selection is fair and suitable alternative employment is offered where it exists or an appropriate redundancy payment is made);
▶   statutory requirements;
▶   some other substantial reason.

The employer must also show s/he acted reasonably in the circumstances, taking into account the employer's size and administrative resources. The dismissal will be unfair if the employer cannot show the above. The detailed provisions are outside the scope of this book.

If a woman is told that she will be made redundant if she is not able to work the required hours, this may be indirect sex discrimination. If it is, it is unlikely to be a 'fair' reason for dismissing the woman and she will also have a claim for unfair dismissal.[12]

Case example

In *Cheal*,[13] two women were told that their part-time jobs were to be replaced by a full-time job. The tribunal found this was 'some other substantial reason' but that the dismissal was unfair. The tribunal was not persuaded that the work could not have been done by the two women and the employers were aware that neither of the women could apply for the job because of their family commitments as mothers of children. Thus the employer had not acted reasonably.

ii   Automatically unfair dismissal

An employer will also be acting unlawfully if s/he dismisses a woman, even if employed for less than two years, because:

a   she is pregnant or for any reason connected with her pregnancy;[14]

b   she has had a baby or for any reason connected with the childbirth and is dismissed during or at the end of maternity leave;[15]

c   she took maternity leave or the benefits of maternity leave and was dismissed after the end of her leave;[16]

d   the employer was required to suspend the woman on health and safety grounds;[17]

e   the woman is redundant and has not been offered suitable alternative employment. Even if it is not possible for a woman to return to the same job because of redundancy, she must be offered any suitable available vacancy. She must be given priority over other redundant employees. Failure to offer suitable available work will make the dismissal automatically unfair;[18]

f   she was sick in the four weeks after the end of maternity leave, having provided the employer with a doctor's certificate, and was dismissed for a reason connected with the birth.[19]

A dismissal in the above circumstances may also be sex discrimination. Although it is important to be aware of these provisions, they are not generally relevant where the claim only relates to a failure to allow a woman to work child friendly working hours. The detailed provisions are outside the scope of this guide.[20]

iii   Constructive Dismissal

This is where an employee terminates her contract (ie resigns), with or without notice, in circumstances where she is entitled to do so because of a significant and fundamental breach of the employment contract by the employer. It is not easy to prove constructive dismissal, and an employee who resigns because she is not allowed to work child friendly hours should, if possible, take advice first. As a guide, the following may entitle the woman to resign and claim constructive dismissal:

▶   where the employer unilaterally changes the employee's hours to her detriment; for example, if she is required to work overtime;

▶   where there is an equal opportunities or maternity policy (where it is incorporated in the contract) which states that applications for jobsharing will be considered and the employer fails to consider them. In *Taylor*,[21] the EAT held that the terms of an equal opportunities policy were part of the contractual rights of the employee, incorporated into his contract of employment. The argument that the policy was only 'a mission statement' was wrong. But in *Grant*,[22] the High Court held that an equal opportunities policy was only a statement of policy, not a contractual obligation (see also *Convery* below);

▶ where there is a breakdown of trust and confidence between employer and employee; this may include the situation where, for example, the employer refuses to discuss with the woman her request for a change in hours or dismisses her request peremptorily (see also *Convery* below);

▶ arguably, a breach of an implied duty not to discriminate would entitle the woman to resign and claim constructive dismissal.

In order to make a claim for constructive dismissal the woman needs to resign without too long a delay. In *Dorrington*,[23] the EAT held that having regard to the employee's length of service and the fact that she needed money for family commitments, the tribunal could properly find that she had not lost her right to resign in response to the employer's breach of contract by delaying a few weeks in order to find alternative work.

Case examples

In *Clay*,[24] the tribunal held that there was indirect sex discrimination when a teacher was not allowed to job-share. The tribunal upheld a complaint of constructive dismissal saying:

> *'With regard to the allegation of constructive dismissal, we are satisfied that the applicant felt, clearly with justification, that there had been unlawful discrimination against her by the respondents. Any employee in these circumstances must therefore feel justified in terminating her employment as the applicant did in this case'.*

In *Convery*[25] the local authority had a job-sharing scheme which provided that 'the presumption of the scheme is that *all* (IT's italics) full-time teaching posts can be made available to job-share'. It also provided that any request to job-share would be 'fully discussed with that employee'. The school did not notify the applicant of the policy, failed to discuss her request with her, and did not, as obliged to do, discuss it with the local authority. The tribunal held that failure to follow the job-share guidelines amounted to a 'serious breach of the implied duty of trust and confidence' and held she was constructively and unfairly dismissed as well as having been discriminated against.

d Unfair, automatically unfair and discriminatory dismissal compared

The main claim where there is failure to allow child-friendly working hours will be for discrimination under the SDA – either that the woman has suffered a detriment or she has been dismissed, usually constructive dismissal.

A claim should also be made for unfair dismissal (and if appropriate automatically unfair dismissal) under the ERA because an SDA dismissal is also likely to be unfair under the ERA. The additional claim is partly because there are different remedies under the ERA and SDA (see p161).

Footnotes

1 *Clarke v Eley Kynock Ltd* [1982] IRLR 482.
2 *Halfpenny v IGE Medical Systems Ltd* EAT 1092/96.
3 *Fairness at Work*, Department of Trade and Industry, CM 3968 (1998).
4 *Crees v Royal London Mutual Insurance Society Ltd v and Greaves v Kwiksave Stores Ltd* [1998] IRLR 245.
5 See footnote 4.
6 ERA s95(1)(a).
7 ERA s95(1)(b).
8 ERA s99(1)(b).
9 ERA s96
10 ERA s95(1)(c). See also SDA s82(1A) which defines constructive discriminatory dismissal and expulsion from a partnership.
11 *R v Secretary of State for Employment ex parte Seymour Smith* [1995] IRLR 464, CA.
12 see footnote 1.
13 *Cheal and Walker v Sussex Alcohol Advice Service* [1994] Case No. 34889/94 and 36691/94 Brighton IT, 23.2.95.
14 ERA s99(1)(a).
15 ERA s99(1)(b).
16 ERA s99(1)(c).
17 ERA s99(1)(d).
18 ERA s99(1)(e).
19 ERA s99(4).
20 *Maternity Rights*, Palmer, C, LAG (1996).
21 *Secretary of State for Scotland v Taylor* [1997] IRLR 608.
22 *Grant v South-West Trains Ltd* [1998] IRLR 188.
23 *Waltons and Morse v Dorrington* [1997] IRLR 488.
24 *Clay v The Governors, English Martyrs School* (1993) Case No. 52310/91 11.1.93 Leicester IT.
25 *Convery v Governers Rawthorpe Infant and Nursery School (1) Kirklees Metropolitan Council (2)* Case No. 1800057/98 Leeds IT

Chapter 15

Procedure for bringing a case

All claims of indirect discrimination (sex and marital) in employment and unfair dismissal must be brought in an employment tribunal.

There are detailed rules which cover the procedure in tribunals.[1] Tribunals have a wide discretion about how to conduct proceedings and may, for example, extend time limits, adjourn the hearing, make orders about documents or witnesses.

Note
Tribunals are usually open to the public and a woman bringing a claim would benefit greatly from watching a tribunal hearing. This will give her an idea of what happens so that it is less intimidating on the day.

1 Informality

The procedure is meant to be informal and accessible to unrepresented parties. If a woman is not represented, the tribunal should help her to understand how to present her claim. If she is represented, whether by a lawyer, adviser or trades union, the tribunal will assume that the representative is familiar with the law and practice. In indirect discrimination cases it is important that a representative is experienced. It is, therefore, often better for a woman to represent herself than be represented by someone who is not familiar with the procedure and law or who only received the papers at the last minute. See Chapter 17 for how to get help and legal advice.

Note

The EOC has produced a step by step guide, 'Taking a Case to an Industrial Tribunal in England and Wales'. This is a very simple straightforward guide with standard forms and precedents. The EOC will send the guide, or extracts, to applicants acting in person. The tribunal also provides free guides.[2]

Remember

If there is a grievance procedure, it is advisable to use this as well as bringing a case. However, it is very important not to miss the time limit for bringing a claim.

2 Letter to employer setting out claim: letter before action

Before lodging a claim, it is usually advisable to write to the employer setting out the nature of the claim. This gives the employer the opportunity to remedy the problem, for example, by allowing child-friendly hours. This is particularly important when the woman is intending to resign if she is not allowed to change her working hours. If there is no reply or a negative one she will then be able to argue that she has been constructively dismissed (see p138).

It is very important that the letter to the employer is accurate, as it may otherwise be used by the employer to show up inconsistencies. The letter should ask for a reply and give a time by which it should come. For examples of letters see Appendix 7.

Remember

Never risk missing the time limit for issuing proceedings.

Remember

There is a duty after dismissal to look for alternative work which is suitable (see p169). Details of attempts to find work should be kept. The costs incurred can be recovered as part of the compensation.

3 The Questionnaire

The questionnaire procedure[3] is very useful for getting information from the employer. It is always worth serving a questionnaire in discrimination cases. It is particularly important in indirect discrimination cases when it is necessary, in order to prove adverse impact, to find out how many women and men, married women and single women, work full and part-time (see p33ff).

There are standard forms which can be obtained from the Job Centre, the EOC or an advice centre.[4] Any question can be asked provided it is relevant to the issues. It is not advisable to ask too many questions as the employer may then say it is oppressive to answer the questionnaire at all. Keep a copy of the complete form. Sample questionnaires are in Appendix 7.

a When can a questionnaire be sent: time limits

A questionnaire can be sent to the employer at any time up to three months from the date of the discrimination. If the employer replies to the questionnaire it may help the woman decide if she has a claim and how to complete the application to the tribunal. However, the lack of response must not delay the woman lodging her Notice of Application, IT1, if the time limit has nearly expired.

If the questionnaire is sent after proceedings have been lodged in the tribunal, it must be sent to the employer within 21 days of that date.

A questionnaire may be sent outside these time limits only with the agreement of the other side or an order from the tribunal. A letter should be sent to the tribunal asking to serve a questionnaire out of time, giving reasons for the delay. Alternatively, it may be raised at a directions hearing if there is one and it will not cause a delay (see p156).

b Second questionnaire

It is possible to send a further questionnaire if the replies to the first one are unclear or raise other questions.[5] Again, the tribunal's permission is needed.

c Does the employer have to reply to the question-naire?

An employer is not obliged to reply to the questionnaire, but if s/he fails to reply for no good reason, delays replying or replies in an evasive or equivocal way, the tribunal can infer that there has been unlawful discrimination.[6] The letter to the employer should point this out. A copy of the questionnaire should also be sent to the tribunal.

Remember

If the employer does not reply, write asking if and when s/he intends to reply.

Sample letter

I refer to my letter of... with which I enclosed a Sex Discrimination Act questionnaire. I do not appear to have received a reply to the question-naire.

You will be aware that if, without reasonable excuse, you do not reply to the questionnaire within a reasonable period, or your reply is evasive or equivocal, the tribunal may draw any inference that it considers it just and equitable to draw, including an inference of unlawful discrimination.

Even if the employer refuses to answer the questionnaire, it is possible to ask similar questions by way of a request for written answers (see below).

d Replies to questionnaire

The replies to the questionnaire will be taken into account by the tribunal.[7] If the replies raise further questions, these can be asked by serving a further questionnaire (see above) or asking for Written Answers (see p151).

4 Time limits for bringing a claim

It is extremely important to bring a claim within the time limits. An applicant must lodge her claim **within** three months of the date of the discrimination.[8] Thus, if the discrimination occurs on 13 June, for example, the claim must be lodged on the 12th or if that is a weekend or holiday, the day immediately prior to that.

However, where the discrimination continues over a period, time only runs from the end of the period.

Note
The tribunal may consider a complaint which is out of time, where it is 'just and equitable' (see below).

a   When does time run?

This depends on whether there was:
▶ a single refusal to allow child-friendly hours, in which case time may run from this date; or
▶ several requests, each of which was considered by the employer and refused, in which case time runs from the date of the last refusal; or
▶ a policy of not allowing child-friendly hours, whether in relation to the workforce, a section of the workforce or the individual job, in which case time runs from the date the policy ceased or the applicant's contract terminated. It is important to distinguish between an act of discrimination with continuing consequences (such as a refusal to recruit) and discrimination extending over a period, such as a policy prohibiting job- sharing.[9]

This is well illustrated by the following case example.

Case example
Mrs Cast asked to job-share before going on maternity leave. She was refused on 30 March 1992. She went on maternity leave on 3 July, gave birth on 12 August and returned to work on 1 March 1993. Mrs Cast repeated her request to job-share in March and on 10 May. The employer wrote saying they had reconsidered her request but could not agree to it. On 7 June 1993 Mrs Cast wrote giving one month's notice of her resignation. Both the tribunal and the EAT held that time ran from the first refusal in March 1992 and she was out of time. The Court of Appeal disagreed saying:[10]
i   where there is a **discriminatory policy**, the time of the employer's refusal to allow a woman to job-share is not relevant. The discrimination is treated as having been committed at the end of the period of the policy (or when the employee's contract comes to an end, eg she

resigns). A policy need not be formal nor in writing; it may be confined to a particular post or role. Thus, there may be a policy relating to one particular applicant. The CA held that there were clearly several decisions about which Mrs Cast complained which indicated the existence of a discriminatory policy in relation to her post. The CA said that time did not run from the date Mrs Cast resigned as this was one of the consequences of the original discriminatory act. Nor did time run from the date the applicant suffered a disadvantage. The CA said that it was not the suffering of detriment which amounted to the indirect discrimination, but the application to her of a requirement, which, whether or not invoked, was to her detriment because she could not comply with it;

ii   where there are **repeated requests** to work child-friendly hours, the three months runs from the date the last request was refused, provided it was reconsidered. It does not matter that the circumstances did not change between each request.[11] If the employer does not consider the request again but merely refers back to and confirms the earlier decision, this will not be a fresh act of discrimination. In Mrs Cast's case the request was reconsidered and so time ran from the last time the request was considered and refused, 10 May, so she had until 9 August to lodge the claim.

b   Practical advice on time limits

Where the employer refuses a request to work child-friendly working hours and does not reconsider a further request, say, when the woman returns from maternity leave, there is a danger that the time limit will run from the date of the first refusal, unless there is a 'policy' not to allow the hours requested – either generally or in relation to the particular job. To be sure of not missing the time limit it is advisable for a woman to issue proceedings within three months from the initial date. However, if she fails to do so, she can make a further request and hope it is reconsidered by the employer, or argue that there is a policy operating. If she is successful in either of these arguments, time will run either from the second refusal or until there is no longer a 'policy'.

It is not easy to identify when a 'policy' exists and it will depend on the circumstances. Useful evidence would include:

▶   if the job had never been done part-time, particularly if there have been previous requests;

▶   where the employer says that the job is not suitable for a part-timer;

► where the employer has said that they will not allow part-time working, job-sharing etc in any jobs.

c   Date of receipt of IT1 by employment tribunal

The relevant date is when the tribunal actually receives the Notice of Application, IT1. The form can be sent to the tribunal by fax or post. The tribunal offices are not usually open during weekends or holidays so if the time limit expires on a day when the office is closed, it may be out of time.

It is advisable to telephone the tribunal to check that the Notice has been received. Even faxes sometimes go astray.

Remember
Make a note of the time limit in a diary immediately. This will avoid the application being out of time. If there is any doubt about when the time limit expires **always** assume that the time limit is the **earliest** date. For example, if the employer says that a woman cannot work part-time, but s/he will check further with another manager and that manager confirms the decision, assume that the time limit runs from the first refusal. However, if, using the earliest date, the time limit has expired, because it was three months or more ago, it is arguable that time runs from the later date (when the other manager confirms the decision).

In order to be safe, it is advisable to lodge the IT1 after the first refusal, or delay making a formal request for child-friendly hours if it would not be practical to take proceedings in the time available. It is difficult to predict whether the tribunal will find that there is a discriminatory policy or that the employer will reconsider the request as opposed to confirming the previous decision.

d   Making a claim out of time

A tribunal may consider a claim made out of time if 'in all the circumstances of the case, it considers that it is just and equitable to do so'.[12] The following may be taken into account:
► the reason for the delay;
► where the woman has a physical or mental illness; a difficult pregnancy or birth will be relevant;
► ignorance as to rights or mistaken belief as to essential matters, provided she has no representative acting for her or advising her;

▶ any disadvantage which may be suffered by the employer as a result of the delay.

The tribunal will want to know why the application is late and a detailed letter should be sent setting out the reasons. The test in discrimination cases for making a claim out of time is much wider than in unfair dismissal claims,[13] where the test is whether it was 'reasonably practicable' to present the complaint in time and it was brought within such time as was reasonable.[14] In *Keeble*, an SDA case,[15] the EAT held that if the only reason for the delay is a wholly understandable misapprehension of the law, that must be a matter which Parliament intended the tribunal to take into account, was relevant and it was just and equitable to extend time.

Remember
It is important for the applicant to:
▶ keep copies of all correspondence with the employer, the questionnaire and all other relevant documents;
▶ keep notes of all important conversations with the employer (including dates).

5 Making an application to the tribunal

The Notice of Application, IT1, must be lodged with the tribunal local to the employer's workplace. It is possible to apply to the tribunal by letter, provided the following information is provided:
▶ the name and address of the applicant,
▶ the name and address of the respondent, and
▶ the grounds of the claim.[16]
However, there is a standard form and it is easier to use this. The application can be faxed to the tribunal. There is no charge for making an application.

a Who to sue

The main respondent will usually be the employer. It is possible to name an individual where s/he has discriminated. In most cases of indirect sex discrimination, this is unlikely to be appropriate as it is generally the organisation as a body which does not allow child-friendly working.

b Amendment of IT1

The IT1 may be amended, either with the agreement of the respondents or with the permission of the tribunal. However, if the amendment changes the basis of the claim, eg from unfair dismissal to discrimination, it may be allowed only if the relevant facts are set out in the IT1. In *Quarcoopome*,[17] the EAT held that a claim for discrimination will include both direct and indirect discrimination and victimisation.

Combined cases

If there are two separate claims and IT1s from the same person which are related to each other they should be heard together. A letter should be written to the tribunal asking for them to be combined. The test is whether:

► there is some common question of law or fact;
► the remedy claimed arises out of the same set of facts; or
► it is otherwise desirable to link them.

The parties must be given notice before an order is made, to allow them to object.[18]

For example

A woman puts in an IT1 complaining of not being allowed to work part-time. She resigns because she could not continue working the long hours and puts in a further IT1 complaining of unfair dismissal. Both claims should be heard together.

6 Employer's reply

The tribunal will send a copy of the IT1 to the employer who then has 21 days to reply. The reply will usually be on form IT3 and this is returned to the tribunal.

Often, the employer will ask for extra time to reply and this is frequently given. The tribunal will send a copy of the employer's reply to the applicant or her representative. (For an example of an IT3 see p207).

7 Advisory, Conciliation and Arbitration Service (ACAS)

All claims are referred to ACAS whose role is to try and reach agreement between the parties.[19] The ACAS officer usually contacts both parties to find out if settlement is possible. S/he must be independent and does not represent either party and so will not advise about whether a settlement is good or not. Discussions with ACAS are confidential and will not be known to the tribunal. Settlements are discussed on p159.

8 Documents

Documentary evidence is often very important in discrimination cases. It is invariably the employer who has most of the relevant documents and the employee will not generally know what documents the employer has.

In tribunal cases there is no automatic right to see relevant documents held by the employer. Tribunals often say that each party must disclose documents on which they intend to rely. However, employers may have documents which are helpful to the employee and which they need not disclose if they themselves do not want to rely on them. This may prejudice the applicant.

There is a procedure, called discovery, whereby the parties can be asked to list and disclose all documents relevant to the claim. The woman should write to the employer (or representative) asking for a list of all documents relevant to the claim. If the employer refuses to provide a list, an application can be made to the tribunal for an order. The test to be applied, in deciding whether disclosure or production of the documents should be ordered, is whether they are relevant to the issues.[20]

If the woman knows or suspects that there are certain categories of documents, for example her personal file, or correspondence between managers about whether her job can be done part-time, she should ask for these documents.

Sample letter to employer

Please confirm that you are prepared to provide full discovery by list, and inspection, as per the county court. In particular, please provide copies of my personal file and all memos relating to my request to change my hours. If I do not hear from you within 14 days, I will apply to the tribunal for an order.

Sample letter to tribunal

We wrote to the respondents on … asking if they were prepared to agree to provide full discovery within 14 days. The respondents say they will only disclose documents on which they intend to rely. I am concerned that if full discovery is not provided this will prejudice me. I am not in a position to know what relevant documents are in the respondent's possession and documents which may help to prove my case may not be disclosed. I would therefore ask for an order for full discovery and inspection as may be ordered in the county court.

Documents from other sources

In indirect discrimination cases it is also important to get information about the labour force showing the number of male and female (married and unmarried women) working full and part-time.

Appendices 4 and 5 contain useful publications and further details of organisations who may provide such information.

9 Request for further and better particulars

Either party can ask for clarification of the other party's case. This can be done by asking for further and better particulars of the IT1 or the IT3.[21] First, a letter should be written to the other side asking for the details. If they are not provided, a letter should be written to the tribunal asking them for an order.

The tribunal will want to be satisfied that the further information is relevant to the case. This is quite a technical procedure and it would be worth getting some advice about how to draft the request (see also Appendix 7 for sample forms).

10 Written answers

Either the employer or employee can make a request for written answers if it would:

- ► help clarify any issue in the proceedings, or
- ► assist the progress of the proceedings for the answer to be made available prior to the hearing (see Appendix 7 for sample questions).[22]

First, a letter setting out the questions should be sent to the employers asking for them to answer the questions. If there is no reply or an inadequate one, a letter should be sent to the tribunal asking for an order.

Note
If there is no reply to the questionnaire, it may be possible to rephrase some of the questions to include in a request for written answers.

11 Failure to comply with a tribunal order: striking out

If either party fails to comply with an order of the tribunal they can be stopped from continuing with the claim, in the case of the applicant, or barred from defending, in the case of the employer.[23]

12 Agreed bundle of documents

It is usual for there to be an agreed bundle of documents for the hearing. Four copies are required for the tribunal, three for the members and one for the witness. A copy will be needed for each party. Usually, it is the applicant's responsibility to prepare the bundles although sometimes the employer will do so. This should be agreed before the hearing. Usually the bundle will consist of:
- ► the pleadings (ie IT1, IT3, Questionnaire and Replies, Further and Better Particulars, Written Answers, Tribunal Orders);
- ► the documents; these may be divided up between:
  - ► documents relevant to the issues (eg memos requesting and refusing child- friendly hours);
  - ► procedures (eg Equal Opportunities Policy, Maternity Policy);
  - ► correspondence between the parties after the issue of proceedings.

Usually, there will be a contents page with each document numbered. Witness statements are usually in a separate bundle but can just be handed in on the day, unless there is an order for exchange, say 14 days before the hearing. Tribunals often like a chronology and *dramatis personae* but these are not essential unless there is an order requiring them.

13 Witnesses

It is important, if possible, for the woman to call witnesses to support her claim. The witness may be another woman who was told she could not work part-time or someone who used to do the job on a part-time basis where it worked very well.

However, it is not usually advisable to call someone to give evidence if they have not provided a written statement or at least indicated what they can and are willing to say. If a witness is still working for the employer s/he will often be unwilling to give evidence against the employer. In these circumstances it is not generally advisable to call her/him.

a   Documents from witnesses

Witnesses can also be asked to bring documents with them.

Witnesses who are still working for the employer often want an order from the tribunal saying that they must attend. A letter should be written to the tribunal requesting a witness order.

Sample letter to tribunal requesting witness order

I have asked... to give evidence on my behalf but she will not attend voluntarily. Her evidence is important because she used to work part-time in my job. I would be grateful if you would make a witness order for her to attend the hearing and bring all documents relating to [her application to work part-time].

The witness order will sometimes be sent to the applicant (or her representative) or direct to the witness. It is important to check that the order has been made.

b Expert witnesses

It can be helpful to call a representative from an organisation such as New Ways to Work who can give evidence about the viability of doing the particular job part-time or job-share. Note, however, that they usually charge about £500.

c Witness statements

It is now quite common for tribunals to ask for or to order witness statements. The statement should set out the detailed facts of the claim in chronological order. If properly prepared, witness statements are very useful. The witness can rely on the statement when giving evidence and will not have to remember all the details of what happened. The evidence will be before the tribunal in an easily accessible form. A sample witness statement is in Appendix 7.

Witness statements may be exchanged before the hearing. If this happens they should be exchanged simultaneously to avoid one party changing their statements in response to what the other party has said.

It is usual for the statement to be read out at the tribunal. Either the witness can add to it as she reads through or her representative may ask some questions to clarify matters.

14 Directions hearings

The tribunal may fix a hearing for directions at which all the above matters, discovery, further and better particulars, written answers, and witness orders may be discussed. In addition, a party who wants to apply for an order, for example, for discovery, may ask for a hearing so that the tribunal can hear the arguments and then decide whether to make an order.

The tribunal may also hold other hearings, before the main one:

a **a preliminary hearing** for the tribunal to decide whether the claim should be heard at all, for example if the claim appears to be out of time;

b **a pre-hearing review** to decide whether the application has any chance of success. If the tribunal decides there is no chance, it may require a deposit of up to £150 as a condition of proceeding.[24]

15 Settlements

Many discrimination claims are settled before the hearing. Settlements are discussed in Chapter 16.

16 The hearing

The tribunal will set a date for the hearing. Some tribunals ask the parties how long they think the hearing will last. This is difficult to estimate, but most cases involving indirect sex discrimination will take at least two days, possibly more.

The tribunal can adjourn a hearing, if, for example:

▶ the case is likely to take longer than it is listed for, or

▶ one of the witnesses (including the employee or employer) is ill or,

▶ the case is not ready for a hearing, particularly if a representative has recently been appointed because, for example, the applicant has just received funding from the EOC.

Order of proceedings

The detail of the hearing is beyond the scope of this book. Usually, however, the order is as follows:

1 The applicant opens by summarising the case, although this is optional and some tribunals prefer to leave out this step.

2 Before giving evidence the applicant must swear on oath or affirm. The applicant will give evidence; if there are written witness statements, she can read the statement and add to it as she goes along. It is also useful to refer to relevant documents.

3 The applicant will be cross-examined by the respondent, ie asked questions about what she has said. The aim of cross-examination is to challenge what the witness has said.

4 The applicant may then be re-examined about anything which arose in cross-examination, if she is represented. If not represented, the applicant may then make a statement relating to the cross-examination.

5 The Tribunal may then ask the applicant some questions.

6 The applicant calls each of her witnesses in turn. If there are witness statements, they will read from them and may be asked supplemen-

tary questions by the applicant. The respondent will cross-examine each witness and the tribunal may also ask questions. The applicant may then re-examine the witness, ie ask questions which came up in the cross-examination.

7   The respondent will then go through the above steps. When the applicant is cross-examining the respondent's witnesses, she must challenge anything with which she disagrees. Failure to do so means that the tribunal will assume that the applicant accepts what the witness has said.

8   The respondent sums up the case in a closing speech.

9   The applicant sums up. This is a chance to summarise the strong points of the case, highlight any inconsistencies in what the respondent, and witnesses said, referring to the documents, and to show why there has been discrimination. In cases of indirect discrimination it is useful to summarise the law, if possible. (See Appendix 7 for example of skeleton argument.)

Advice to witnesses

▶   if you cannot remember exactly what happened, don't guess. It is much worse to guess and then be proved wrong than to say you cannot remember but think that something happened. However, if you can infer what happened from what you do remember, you can explain this;

▶   do not make categorical statements unless you are sure they are true;

▶   make sure you answer the question asked and keep the answer short and to the point, if possible;

▶   you should not be asked 'leading questions' by the person questioning you. Leading questions involve telling the witness what to say. An example is 'The employer told you the job could easily be done part-time, didn't he?'. Instead the question should be 'What did the employer tell you?'. Leading questions can be, and usually are, asked in cross-examination.

17   Tribunal's decision

The tribunal does not always make a decision immediately. It may take weeks and will be sent in the post to the applicant and respondent or their representatives.

18 Review

There is a right to a review within 14 days if, for example, new evidence has become available since the conclusion of the hearing which could not have been foreseen, the interests of justice require a review or for other technical reasons which are outside the scope of this book.[25]

19 Appeals

There is a right to an appeal, on a point of law, to the Employment Appeal Tribunal, within 42 days of the date of the decision. There is a further appeal to the Court of Appeal and then to the House of Lords. This is beyond the scope of this book.

20 Reference to the European Court of Justice (ECJ)

Any tribunal or court may refer a point of European law to the ECJ. This is done by way of asking specific questions of law. The ECJ will answer these, giving reasons, and the case will be sent back to the referring tribunal or court to make a decision on the facts.

21 Expenses

A claim can be made for the applicant and witnesses for the costs of travel, meals and loss of earnings. The clerk will provide a form and advise about a claim.

22 Costs

The usual rule in the ET and EAT is that neither party pays the costs of the other side. A tribunal can only make an order that one party pays the costs if they have acted 'frivolously, vexatiously or unreasonably'.[26]

Remember

Legal aid is available for the EAT subject to means and merits. In the Court of Appeal the costs of the winner are paid by the loser.

Footnotes

1 The Industrial Tribunal (Constitution and Rules of Procedure) Regulations 1993 SI No 2687 (referred to as the IT rules).
2 *Understanding Industrial Tribunals – What do Industrial Tribunals do; Understanding Industrial Tribunals – How to apply to an Industrial Tribunal; Understanding Industrial Tribunals – Hearings at Industrial Tribunals; A Section 74 Questionnaire.* All available from local tribunals.
3 SDA s74.
4 *Sex Discrimination* (Questions and Replies) Order 1975 SI No 2048.
5 *Carrington v Helix Lighting Ltd* [1990] IRLR 6, EAT.
6 SDA s74(2)(b).
7 SDA s74.
8 SDA s76(1).
9 *Owusu v London Fire & Civil Defence Authority* [1995] IRLR 574 EAT.
10 *Cast v Croydon College* [1997] IRLR 14.
11 The CA in Cast held that the decision in *Rovenska v General Medical Council* [1997] IRLR 367 did not mean that a decision following consideration of a repetition of an earlier request can only amount to an act of discrimination in its own right if the further request contains fresh material.
12 SDA s76(5).
13 *Hawkins v Ball and Barclays Bank plc* [1996] IRLR 258.
14 ERA s111.
15 *BCC v Keeble* [1997] IRLR 337 EAT. See also *Mills and Crown Prosecution Service v Marshall* EAT 11.2.98 (528/97)
16 IT Regs Sch 1 rule 1.
17 *Quarcoopome v Sock Shop Holdings Ltd* [1995] IRLR 353.
18 IT Regs Sch 1 rule 18.
19 SDA s64(1).
20 IT Regs Sch 1 rule 4((1) and County Court Rules Order 14 r11(1) and 8(1).
21 IT Regs Sch 1 rule 4(1)(a).
22 The Industrial Tribunal (Constitution and Rules of Procedure) Regulations 1993 Sch 1 rule 4(3).
23 IT Regs Sch 1 r13.
24 Industrial Tribunals Act 1996, s9.
25 IT Regs Sch 1 rule 10.
26 IT Regs Sch 1 rule 12.

Chapter 16

Remedies and compensation

The woman making a claim must be clear what she wants from the proceedings and how far she is prepared to take them. This will determine how negotiations are conducted and whether and when legal proceedings are issued (see p105). Some women feel that a good reference is the most important remedy as, without that, it may be difficult to find alternative work. This will only be available through a negotiated settlement. On the other hand, if maximum compensation is the priority, this is most likely to be achieved through issuing legal proceedings.

There are different remedies for a discrimination claim under the Sex Discrimination Act and an unfair dismissal claim under the Employment Rights Act. Where there has been a dismissal a claim should be made under both Acts. Generally, a dismissal which is discriminatory will also be unfair. In *Clarke*,[1] the EAT said that it did not follow, as a matter of law, that an indirectly discriminatory dismissal was an unfair one, but that it would need very special circumstances to find such a dismissal fair. Compensation is likely to be higher for discrimination and the recoupment (of benefit) rules do not apply (see p168).

1 Settlement

Settlement which then prevents the woman making a claim to the tribunal can only be made through ACAS or a lawyer or a relevant independent adviser.

For example

If the employer says to a woman 'take £1,000 in settlement of any claim you may have', and she takes the money, she can still bring proceedings for discrimination within the three month period. Similarly, any money for redundancy can be accepted without affecting the woman's right to sue.

a   ACAS

If there is a settlement through ACAS, the terms will be incorporated on a form called COT3, which must be signed by both applicant and respondent, or their representatives. This is binding on both parties and enforceable.

It is common for agreement to be reached just before the hearing. If oral agreement is reached between the parties and ACAS, this is likely to be binding even before the COT3 is signed (see p213 for sample COT3).

b   Settlement through a relevant independent adviser

A claim for unfair dismissal or discrimination can only be settled without ACAS if the applicant has received legal advice from a relevant independent adviser and there is a written agreement. The requirements are that:

▶   the legal advice must explain the terms and effect of the agreement;
▶   the legal advice must explain what the settlement means, ie that the claim cannot be pursued in a tribunal or other court;
▶   the relevant independent adviser must be covered by professional negligence insurance;
▶   the agreement must be in writing; oral agreement is not sufficient;
▶   the agreement must relate only to the particular complaint;
▶   the agreement must identify the particular relevant independent adviser who has advised the employee; and
▶   the agreement must state that the conditions relating to compromise agreements under the relevant Acts are satisfied.[2]

2 Different remedies available for discrimination and unfair dismissal

The remedy available will depend on the claim made. The table below summarises the position:

Discrimination	Unfair dismissal
No basic award	Basic award
Compensation with no ceiling – not subject to recoupment	Compensation with £12,000 ceiling. subject to recoupment of benefits (at April 1998)
Compensation for injury to feelings	No compensation for injury to feelings
No order for reinstatement or re-engagement as such	Order for reinstatement or re-engagement with extra compensation payable in default
Recommendation: Extra award may be made in default	No recommendation
Interest payable on injury to feelings from date of discrimination. For existing loss of earnings payable from midway point.	No interest payable unless compensation not paid within 42 days.
Declaration of discrimination	No declaration

Note

A woman will only get a good reference if the employer agrees. It is therefore better to negotiate this through settlement. However, failure to provide a reference because a woman has brought proceedings will be victimisation (see ECJ decision in *Coote v Granada Hospitality Ltd* 22.9.98 ECJ case c-185/97).

a   Compensation

Most applicants want compensation. Unlike claims for unfair dismissal where the ceiling, in October 1998, is £12,000,[3] in sex discrimination claims, whether direct or indirect, there is no ceiling. For summaries of recent awards and settlements, see p166.

An employee can claim the following losses:

i   loss of earnings up to the date of the tribunal hearing;
ii   loss of future earnings;
iii   loss of opportunity;

iv   loss of benefits, such as pension, car allowance, health insurance, maternity benefits;

v   expenses incurred in looking for alternative work;

vi   special damages, such as the cost of paying for psychotherapy;

vii injury to feelings;

viii aggravated damages;

ix   interest.

Basis on which order is made

Tribunals can make an order where it is 'just and equitable to do so',[4] but the amount of compensation is not limited by this principle.

The aim of compensation is to put the applicant into the position she would have been in, but for the unlawful conduct, ie she can recover all foreseeable loss arising from the discrimination.[5] Although in *Cannock*,[6] the EAT said that tribunals should have a sense of proportion in awarding compensation, subsequent EAT decisions have confirmed that:

> *even if the individual has suffered a substantial loss, it is the duty of the tribunal to award that loss as compensation so as to ensure that the loss and damage actually sustained as a result of the discriminatory dismissal is made good in full.*[7]

Compensation in indirect sex discrimination

Prior to 1996 there was no power to order compensation in cases of indirect discrimination. This has now changed so that compensation can be awarded.[8] Where the indirect discrimination is 'unintentional' – ie the employer did not appreciate the discriminatory affect of the requirement or condition, the tribunal can order compensation:

a   if it would have made a declaration or recommendation when there was no power to order compensation (ie prior to 25 March 1996), or

b   where it does make a declaration or recommendation and it considers it just and equitable to order compensation as well.

In practice, most employers should now be aware of the discriminatory effect of child-unfriendly working hours and, if not, this should have been brought to their attention by the employee when she asks to work child-friendly hours.

Note
If a woman resigns and then finds a better paid job with at least equivalent benefits, she will have no loss under heads (i) to (iv) above. However, she will still have a claim for injury to feelings and possibly aggravated damages.

i   Loss of earnings: loss up to date of hearing
In order to calculate loss up to the date of the hearing:
▶ work out the amount earned in the previous job for the period in question, net of tax; include any pay increase or bonus which would have been received;
▶ deduct the amount earned in the new job over a similar period.

ii   Future loss
This is more difficult to calculate, particularly where the woman has resigned or been dismissed. It involves assessing:
▶ how long it will take the woman to find another job, taking into account her age and skills,
▶ availability of work on a part-time basis,
▶ the local job market for the type of work,
▶ what she is likely to get paid,
▶ promotion prospects at the last job and future promotion prospects,
▶ whether a woman, who did not return from maternity leave, would have returned had she been allowed to work child-friendly hours,
▶ the effect of having a young baby on a woman's job prospects,
▶ childcare costs.

Remember
If a woman has resigned because she was not allowed to work part-time, her loss will be based on the maximum number of hours she was prepared to work.

Assessing compensation in pregnancy dismissals
In pregnancy dismissal cases the tribunal will first decide whether the woman would have returned to work had she not been dismissed. In *Cannock*, the EAT held that tribunals should assess this as a percentage chance, so that if there was a 50% chance of her returning, she would receive 50% of her earnings. The percentage deduction should be applied **after** mitigation has been taken into account.

If a woman is told she cannot work child-friendly hours and resigns before going on maternity leave, the tribunal may consider what would have happened if she had been allowed to return part-time. Arguably, where a woman makes it clear that she would like to return on reduced hours, the assumption must be that this is what she would have done and no reduction should be made.

Childcare costs

The tribunal will deduct the full cost of childcare rather than assume that the woman's partner will pay half. Arguably, this is wrong. Surely, an assumption that only women and not men pay for childcare is in itself discriminatory?

iii   Loss of work and loss of opportunity

Where there is a failure to recruit or promote because, for example, the employer insists on child-unfriendly hours, the woman should be compensated for the loss of a valuable chance to obtain work. Relevant factors will be:

▶   the likelihood that the woman would have obtained the job, if there had been no discrimination,

▶   how long she would have stayed in the job,

▶   how long it will take the woman to find alternative work.

Where the woman has subsequently obtained a better paid job, she may be awarded an amount for loss of opportunity if the job which she was refused would have offered better promotion prospects.

iv   Loss of benefits

There may be benefits which have been lost and these can be claimed, among them:

▶   profit-related pay,

▶   pension,

▶   company car,

▶   health insurance,

▶   professional subscriptions.

Pension loss

The calculation of pension loss can be very complicated. There are guidelines for tribunal chairs on assessment of loss on pension rights. However, the EAT has held that these may not be appropriate in discrimination cases where there is no ceiling on compensation. The actual loss may well be greater than the employer's contributions. Where it is substantial, it may be worth getting advice from an actuary who can also be called to give evidence to the tribunal.

v Expenses incurred in looking for work

Fares, telephone calls, travel, photocopying costs, which are incurred in seeking work, can be recovered. All receipts, tickets, telephone bills etc should be kept and must be produced if a claim is to be made.

vi Special damages

This may include fees for psychotherapy where a woman has suffered anxiety and stress as a result of the employer's behaviour.

vii Injury to feelings

An amount for injury to feelings can be awarded in sex discrimination cases. Although an award is not made automatically, the EAT have said in *Murray*,[9] that 'in our view, it is almost inevitable in sex discrimination cases that a claim for hurt feelings be made'. The award can include an amount for loss of 'congenial employment'.

The main principles behind the award were laid down in *Johnson*,[10] a race discrimination case, but also apply to sex discrimination cases:

▶ the aim is to compensate the applicant fully, not to punish the discriminator;

▶ awards should not be so low as this would diminish respect for the anti-discrimination laws. Nor should they be too high that they are seen as untaxed riches;

▶ awards should be similar to the range of awards in personal injury cases;

▶ tribunals should bear in mind the value in everyday life of the sums they are awarding and the need for public respect for the level of awards.

The tribunal should take account of the degree of upset suffered by the applicant.

viii Aggravated damages

Aggravated damages may be awarded where the employer has behaved in a high-handed, malicious, insulting or oppressive manner in committing the act of discrimination.[11] The tribunal may take into account:

- unsatisfactory answers to a questionnaire;[12]
- failure to investigate a complaint of discrimination;[13]
- the way a grievance was investigated, particularly if a complaint of discrimination is not taken seriously; in *Johnson*, the employer said that the applicant thought all white people were racists and blamed his problems on non-existent discrimination, the applicant was awarded £7,500;
- the way the employers conduct the case, if, for example, the honesty of the applicant is attacked during the hearing.[14]

ix   Interest

Interest is payable on injury to feelings awards from the date of the discriminatory act to the date of the decision. In relation to other awards, apart from future losses, it is paid from a date midway between the date of the discrimination and the date of the decision.[15] It may be awarded in relation to a different period where there are exceptional circumstances.

In addition, interest is payable on discrimination awards from the day after the decision until it is paid, unless the award is paid in full within 14 days of the decision, in which case interest is not payable.

Examples of awards

The following are some examples of tribunal orders. The amount payable will depend on the woman's earnings.

Facts

In *Tickle*,[16] the applicant worked part-time on a series of fixed term contracts. She was told her contract would not be renewed as the Governors wanted a full-time person. The IT found that she made a reasoned and legitimate decision that she could not work full-time until her youngest child was at school and the requirement to work full-time was not justified.

Mrs Tickle had found another job but had to travel further and work longer hours so had increased childminding and travel costs.

Order

a   Reinstatement;

b   extra childminding and travel costs for a year, less any additional sums which she earned in the new job;

c   £4,000 for general damages (ie non-pecuniary loss) including injury to feelings.

Facts

In *Given*,[17] the applicant, an Implementation Team member, asked to job-share and was told that it was a non-starter at her level. She was told that other options such as a career break, part-time working, job-share or voluntary selective severance were not available. Mrs Given returned to work after her maternity leave and again raised the issue of job-share but was refused. She resigned. The tribunal found there was indirect sex and marriage discrimination.

Mrs Given obtained another job but at a lower rate.

Order

a   Five years compensation on the basis she could return to work when her children were of school-age; this consisted of £3,000 past loss of earnings and £27,000 future loss;

b   £5,000 injury to feelings.

Facts

In *Cheal*,[18] two part-time secretaries/receptionists were replaced by a full-time worker. The tribunal found that the applicants had been subjected to a detriment because they could not apply for their job because of the requirement to work full-time and that led to their dismissal.

Order

a   Loss of net pay for 26 weeks; she found another job after 26 weeks;

b   Cost of re-training (£465);

c   Expenses in going for interviews (£120);

d   Failure to give adequate reasons for dismissal (£168.46);

e   Loss of statutory and industrial rights (£150).

These orders were made under the unfair dismissal legislation, the details of which are outside the scope of this book.

Facts

In *Gold*,[19] the applicant was not promoted because she was job-sharing.

Order

a   Recommendation that the applicant be considered for promotion;

b   £6,000 for injury to feelings.

Facts

In *Roberts and Longstaffe*,[20] the applicants took maternity leave during 1994 and asked to job-share on their return. The requests were refused.

Order

a   Recommendation that both applicants should be allowed to job share by 11 March 1995;

b   Injury to feelings: £500 to both applicants.

Facts

In *Stimpson*,[21] the applicant was a receptionist/telephonist and asked to work part-time or job-share. She was refused and the tribunal found this to be indirectly discriminatory.

Recommendations:

a   Recommendation that the respondents consult with ACAS and the EOC as to the formulation of an Equal Opportunities Policy;

b   The respondents give consideration to their procedures to ensure that employment interviews be minuted.

Order

a   Economic loss over 26 weeks;

b   Injury to feelings of £1,000;

c   Interest.

Other settlements for refusal to allow job-share or part-time work

Andrews v Globe Nursery School 1996	£10,250
French v Bank of America 1996	£20,000
Rolls v IPC Magazines 1996	£35,000
Schofield v Zurich Insurance	£20,000[22]

Unfortunately the women's salaries are not known.

Recoupment

Compensation for unfair dismissal is subject to the recoupment rules, whereby the State will recover social security benefits where compensation has been paid for the same period. This does **not** apply to compensation for discrimination. Where a woman is claiming a benefit, it is therefore better that compensation be awarded for discrimination, not unfair dismissal. The recoupment rules do not apply to any settlements.

3 Employee must look for alternative work: duty to mitigate

Where a woman has been dismissed or has resigned, she must take steps to look for another job. She has a duty to mitigate her loss. Failure to do so is likely to reduce the compensation she receives if the tribunal find she could have found other work. Evidence of steps she has taken should be kept, including:

▶ copies of job applications,
▶ notes of interviews,
▶ visits to the job centre, and
▶ details of conversations with recruitment agencies.

The costs of looking for work can be recovered in the compensation provided there is evidence of the loss (see p165).

It is up to the employer to show, by producing evidence, that the woman has failed to mitigate her loss. An assertion that she has failed to look for work is not sufficient.[23]

A woman who has resigned from a job because she cannot work the required hours should not be expected to take a job which also requires child-unfriendly hours.

Failure to mitigate

If the tribunal finds that the woman has failed to mitigate her loss, the compensation will be reduced to reflect this.

Note

The calculation should be as follows:[24]

a   take the amount the woman would have earned in her previous job; say it was £500 per week;

b   deduct from that the sum she should have earned if she had mitigated her loss properly; say, she should have earned £400 per week;

c   then discount that net sum by the appropriate percentage to reflect the chance she might not have remained in her old job; say, there was a 90% chance she would have remained.

▶ £500 – £400 = £100;
▶ 90% of £100 = £90;
▶ Her loss per week is £90.

4 Declaration

This is a statement by the tribunal declaring that the applicant has suffered unlawful discrimination.[25] By itself, it does not lead to compensation or any other remedy.

5 Recommendation

The tribunal can make a recommendation that, within a specified time period, the employer take some action to remove or reduce the effect of the discrimination on the applicant.[26] The recommendation must relate to the applicant; the order cannot require the employer to cease a discriminatory practice. However, tribunals often make general, but unenforceable, recommendations to this effect.

a   Types of recommendation

The tribunal could order, for example, that:
▶   the woman be allowed to reduce her hours or job-share;
▶   she be able to work at home for part of the time;
▶   she be able to take a shorter lunch break and leave earlier.

Case example

In *Hicks*,[27] the tribunal recommended that a full-time teacher be allowed to return on a part-time basis after maternity leave and with a pro rata salary. In *Robertson* and *Griffith*,[28] the tribunal recommended that the applicants' contracts be amended so they should work a 35 hour fortnight instead of week.

In *Noone*,[29] the EAT held that a tribunal cannot recommend that the woman be appointed to the next available post as this was positive discrimination.

Although there is no power, under the SDA, to order reinstatement or re-engagement, arguably the power to make a recommendation could include such an order. This has yet to be tested.

b   Failure to comply with a recommendation

If the employer does not comply with a recommendation, and cannot justify the failure, the tribunal may increase the amount of compensation payable or make an order for compensation, if none was made originally.[30]

6 Unfair dismissal remedies

Where a woman has been dismissed or resigned and is claiming constructive dismissal, she should make a claim for ordinary and automatically unfair dismissal (for distinction see p161).
She can claim:

a   **the basic award**, consisting of
   ▶   half a week's gross pay for each of the years worked while under the age of 22;
   ▶   one week's gross pay for the years in which the worker was between the ages of 22 and 40;
   ▶   one-and-a-half week's gross pay for each year when the employee was 41 or more, until she reaches 65.
   The week's pay is subject, at April 1998, to a maximum limit of £220 gross per week and a maximum of 20 years continuous employment can be taken into account.[31]

b   **a compensatory award**, which is payable for loss of earnings and benefits; this is not paid twice for both unfair dismissal and discrimination. At present there is a statutory limit to the size of the award of £12,000. The limit is likely to be removed by the end of 1999.

c   **reinstatement and re-engagement**; reinstatement is where the woman is given her job back and re-engagement is where she is re-employed in a different job.[32] An order will only be made where it would be practicable; if the woman has been replaced an order is unlikely to be made.

d   **interest on compensation** is payable if the compensation is not paid within 42 days of the order.[34]

Note
If the employer refuses to comply with an order, an additional award of compensation can be made. This is between 13 and 26 weeks'

pay in unfair dismissal cases in addition to the maximum award, and between 26 and 52 weeks' pay in sex discrimination cases.33

7 Costs

Costs are not normally awarded in the tribunal unless one of the parties has acted frivolously, vexatiously, abusively, disruptively or otherwise unreasonably in bringing or conducting the proceedings.35 Employers often threaten costs but these are rarely awarded.

8 Tax on awards and settlements

a Awards

The basic award and redundancy payment is tax free.

The compensatory award is tax free because the loss is awarded net of tax.36

Arguably, injury to feelings should not be taxable because it is similar to personal injury awards.

b Settlements

Sums received for loss of office or employment, including any statutory redundancy payment or basic award, is tax free up to the value of £30,000.37 Arguably, injury to feelings should be tax free.

Payments in respect of contractual loss, such as notice payments, unpaid wages, loss of earnings or commission are taxable as income received from the job.

Note
If the settlement is substantial, it is advisable to take professional advice on the tax implications.

Footnotes

1 *Clarke v Eley (IMI) Kynoch Ltd* [1982] IRLR 482.
2 ERA s203, SDA S77(4A) as awarded by Employment Rights (Dispute Resolution) Act 1998 s11, which enables certified trades union officers or members or certified advice workers to sign compromise agreements.
3 ERA s124(1).
4 SDA s65(1)(b).
5 SDA s66(4).
6 *Ministry of Defence v Cannock and others* 1994 IRLR 509.
7 *MOD v Bristow* (24.7.95) and *MOD v Hunt and Others* [1996] IRLR 139.
8 SI 1996/438.
9 *Murray v Powertech* (Scotland) Ltd [1992] IRLR 257.
10 *ARG Armitage, Marsden and HM Prison Service v Johnson* [1997] IRLR 162.
11 *Alexander v Home Office* [1988] IRLR 190.
12 *Bradford City MC v Arora* [1991] ICR 226.
13 *Chan v LB Hackney* (1997) 31 DCLD.
14 *Bamber v Fuji International Finance plc* [1991] ICR 226, though this is only a tribunal decision.
15 Industrial Tribunal (Interest on Awards in Discrimination Cases) Regulations 1996 SI No 2803.
16 *Tickle v Governors of Riverview CF School* Case No. 32420/92 D4160 8.7.94.
17 *Given v Scottish Power plc* Case No. S/3172 94 (1995) 24 EOR DCLD.
18 *Cheal v Sussex Alcohol Advice Service* Case No. 33889/94 and 36691/94 Brighton IT 9.3.95.
19 *Gold v London Borough of Tower Hamlets* Case No. 05608/91/LN/C; London (North) 21.12.94.
20 *Roberts and Longstaffe v British Telecommunications plc* Case Nos. 37399/94 and 40221/94 Southampton IT 11.1.95.
21 *Stimpson v The Dewjoc Partnership* Case No. 61562/94; Middlesborough IT 13.9.95.
22 EOR 76 November/December 1997, p4.
23 *Ministry of Defence v Hunt and Others* [1996] ICR 554 EAT.
24 *Ministry of Defence v Wheeler* [1998] IRLR 23.
25 SDA s65(1)(a).
26 SDA s56(1)(c).
27 *Hicks v North Yorkshire CC* COIT 1643/17.
28 *Robertson and Griffith v Strathclyde Regional Council* S/3332/85 & S/3555/85; Glasgow IT 29.1.86.
29 *Noone v North West Thames Regional Health Authority* (No.2) [1988] IRLR 530 CA. See also *Scottish Agricultural College v O'Mara* (1991) 5 November, DCLD 12, Case No, AT/449/91.
30 SDA s63(5).
31 ERA s227(1)(a); this amount applies from 1.4.98.
32 ERA s94 and ss113 to 115.
33 ERA s117.
34 Industrial Tribunals (Interest) Order 1991 SI No 479.
35 IT Regs Sch 1 r12.
36 *Ministry of Defence v Mutton* [1996] ICR 590.
37 Income and Corporation Taxes Act 1988, s148.

Chapter 17

Legal advice and funding a claim

It is often very difficult to obtain advice and assistance to make a discrimination claim and many solicitors and advisers are not familiar with the law.

1 Advice and assistance from voluntary organisations

Free advice and assistance may be available from voluntary organisations, such as:
▶ the Maternity Alliance,
▶ Mary Ward Legal Centre (which covers Greater London),
▶ Citizens' Advice Bureaux (CABs),
▶ Law Centres,
▶ Rights of Women (ROW),
▶ Bar Pro Bono Unit,
▶ Free Representation Unit (FRU).

The addresses and telephone numbers are in Appendix 4.

The Maternity Alliance

Maternity Alliance has an information line for women wanting advice about any aspect of maternity law, including the right to argue for child-friendly working hours. Women can also write to Maternity Alliance for a leaflet. The Maternity Alliance does not usually take on cases but has a list of advice agencies and solicitors who are experienced in indirect sex discrimination cases.

Law Centres

Law Centres provide free, specialist legal help. There are relatively few in the country (about 50). They generally only give advice and act for people who live or work in their catchment area and often only advise those who are on low incomes. Many, but not all, have experienced employment advisers. If there is a law centre in the area, they should be the first point of contact.

Citizens' Advice Bureaux

CABs provide basic information on all aspects of employment law. Some have expertise in discrimination, but many do not. If they do not, the CAB should be able to provide details of other agencies or solicitors.

Rights of Women

ROW has an advice line with experienced lawyers who can provide advice on discrimination.

Bar Pro Bono Unit

This consists of a group of barristers (about 650) who will advise and represent applicants on short cases (up to three days) for no fee. Applicants must complete an application form which is considered by a member of the Unit according to the merits, the income of the applicant, and the availability of legal aid.

However, one word of warning. If the barrister is unavailable at the last moment, because s/he is in another case which has run over, although the Unit will try and find a replacement, they cannot guarantee to do so.

Free Representation Unit

FRU, which is based in London and Liverpool, usually only takes referrals from agencies with whom they have links, mainly Citizens' Advice Bureaux. Representation is usually by pupil barristers and solicitors and those who have recently started work as barristers.

2 The Equal Opportunities Commission (EOC)

The EOC can give advice or financial assistance which may include:

▶ giving advice on individual complaints,

▶ helping to complete the IT1, questionnaire, request for further and better particulars and other documents,

▶ negotiating a settlement,

▶ arranging for representation, for example by themselves, or a solicitor or barrister,

▶ any other form of assistance they consider appropriate.[1]

The EOC take on very few individual cases. They are only likely to do so if the case will:

▶ clarify important points of law or principle;

▶ affect a large number of people;

▶ bring about change;

▶ be successful;

▶ provide the EOC with follow-up work.

However, even if the EOC does not take on a case, they will often give advice and help with drafting. They have a number of publications which may be sent to applicants without charge. They also have a list of solicitors and advice agencies who can help.

3 Trades Unions

A trades union may be prepared to advise and assist a member. Either the local representative or the full-time officer should be approached for help. Unions also have lawyers who can advise on difficult cases. They may also have equal opportunities officers who can help.

Many advice agencies will want to know if the union has been contacted before taking on a case. The union may be able to negotiate on the woman's behalf and this can be very helpful. In a few cases the union can pay for a lawyer to represent the woman.

4 Legal expenses insurance

Some women have legal costs insurance which is added on to their or their partner's or family's mortgage, house or car insurance, credit card or other insurance policy. With some policies it is free of charge and with others there is a small charge, often about £12-£15 per year. Most policies cover employment matters, although many exclude equal pay.

There are generally conditions attached to the policy such as:

▶ a waiting period between taking out the policy and making a claim; it is not possible to take out the insurance after the claim has arisen;

▶ a requirement to inform the insurance company of the claim as soon as it arises or within a specified period;

▶ a requirement to pay the first £50 (or similar sum) of the solicitor's costs.

Right to choose your own solicitor

There are legal provisions which state that the insured person has a right to choose her own solicitor. The Regulations provide: 'Where, under a legal expense insurance contract, recourse is had to a lawyer … to defend, represent or serve the interests of the insured in any enquiry or proceedings, the insured shall be free to choose that lawyer.' Breach is an offence under the Insurance Companies Act 1982.[2] Many insurance companies try very hard to dissuade clients from using a solicitor of their choice as they prefer to instruct in-house lawyers or solicitors from their panel. For example:

▶ some tell clients that they have no right to choose a solicitor; this is wrong and an offence; a complaint can be made to the insurance ombudsman;

▶ others say that cover will not be provided until proceedings have been issued unless the client uses the in-house solicitors.

5 Legal Aid

If the woman is on a very low income, including income support or family credit she may be able to get a lawyer to advise her under the 'green form' scheme. Initially, only two hours of advice is allowed but this may be extended. There is no limit to the number of extensions which may be obtained but cover does not extend to preparation for the hearing nor representation.

Legal Aid is, however, available for an appeal to the EAT, subject to a financial and merits test.

Where a woman recovers money as a result of the case, it must be repaid to the Legal Aid Board up to the amount spent on legal costs.

Remember

Each party pays its own costs so there is little risk of having to pay the employer's costs in either the ET or EAT (see p157).

6 Contingency fees: no win, no fee

With employment tribunal proceedings, solicitors can take a case on the basis that if the case is lost, there will be no fee to the solicitor and if won, the fees will come out of the compensation. The rules prohibiting contingency fees only apply to 'contentious' matters. Employment tribunal proceedings are defined as 'non-contentious' so the rules do not apply.[3] However, there is likely to be a significant uplift on the normal fees charged in order to compensate the solicitor for the risk. The solicitor may also take a percentage of the compensation and there should be a written agreement covering this. Barristers are now also allowed to do cases on a 'no win, no fee' basis.

Footnotes

[1] SDA s75(2).

[2] The Insurance Companies (Legal Expenses Insurance) Regulations (1990).

[3] Solicitors Practice Rules r8.

Appendices

Extracts from:
Sex Discrimination Act 1975

1   Discrimination to which Act applies

(1) A person discriminates against a woman in any circumstances relevant for the purposes of any provision of this Act if –

(a)   on the ground of her sex he treats her less favourably than he treats or would treat a man, or

(b)   he applies to her a requirement or condition which he applies or would apply equally to a man but –

    i   which is such that the proportion of women who can comply with it is considerably smaller than the proportion of men who can comply with it, and

    ii   which he cannot show to be justifiable irrespective of the sex of the person to whom it is applied, and

    iii   which is to her detriment because she cannot comply with it.

(2) If a person treats or would treat a man differently according to the man's marital status, his treatment of a woman is for the purposes of subsection (1)(a) to be compared to his treatment of a man having the like marital status.

2   Sex discrimination against men

(1) Section 1, and the provisions of Parts II and III relating to sex discrimination against women, are to be read as applying equally to the treatment of men, and for that purpose shall have effect with such medications as are requisite.

(2) In the application of subsection (1) no account shall be taken of special treatment afforded to women in connection with pregnancy or childbirth.

3   Discrimination against married persons

(1) A person discriminates against a married person of either sex in any circumstances relevant for the purposes of any provision of Part II if –

(a)   on the ground of his or her marital status he treats that person less favourably than he treats or would treat an unmarried person of the same sex, or

(b)   he applies to that person a requirement or condition which he applies or would apply equally to an unmarried person but

(i)   which is such that the proportion of married persons who can comply with it is considerably smaller than the proportion of unmarried persons of the same sex who can comply with it, and

(ii)   which he cannot show to be justifiable irrespective of the marital status of the person to whom it is applied, and

(iii)   which is to that person's detriment because he cannot comply with it.

(2) For the purposes of subsection (1), a provision of Part II framed with reference to discrimination against women shall be treated as applying equally to the treatment of men, and for that purpose shall effect with such modifications as are requisite.

6   Discrimination against applicants and employees

(1) It is unlawful for a person, in relation to employment by him at an establishment in Great Britain, to discriminate against a woman:

(a)   in the arrangements he makes for the purpose of determining who should be offered that employment, or

(b)   in the terms on which he offers her that employment, or

(c)   by refusing or deliberately omitting to offer her that employment.

(2) It is unlawful for a person, in the case of a woman employed by him at an establishment in Great Britain, to discriminate against her –

(a) in the way he affords her access to opportunities for promotion, transfer or training, or to any other benefits, facilities or services, or by refusing or deliberately omitting to afford her access to them, or

(b) by dismissing her, or subjecting her to any other detriment.

82 General interpretation provisions

(1) "employment" means employment under a contract of service or of apprenticeship or a contract personally to execute any work or labour, and related expressions shall be construed accordingly.

(1a) A References in this Act to the dismissal of a person from employment or to the expulsion of a person from a position as partner include references –

(a) to the termination of that person's employment or partnership by the expiration of any period (including a period expiring by reference to an event or circumstance), not being a termination immediately after which the employment or partnership is renewed on the same terms; and

(b) to the termination of that person's employment or partnership by any act of his (including the giving of notice) in circumstances such that he is entitled to terminate it without notice by reason of the conduct of the employer or, as the case may be, the conduct of the other partners.

EC childcare
good-practice guide
(reproduced from Equal Opportunities Review 77)

Guidance* on implementing the 1992 Council Recommendation on childcare (92/241/EEC), EOR 43, has been issued by the European Commission (EC). It is intended "as a tool, to be used both separately and in partnership, by government at all levels, social partners, and practitioners, to help them translate policy into effective practice."

Though non-binding, the Recommendation is a benchmark for an effective childcare system. It calls for action to improve the provision of childcare services, for leave for employed parents of both sexes, for measures to make workplaces more supportive of parents, and for more equal sharing of family responsibilities between women and men. The EC guide Work and childcare: a guide to good practice "is designed to supplement the Recommendation by providing detailed suggestions for how it might be implemented," says Social Affairs Commissioner Padraig Flynn.

The guide comprises four chapters:

► Chapter one, "Working and caring: reconciling work and family responsibilities", describes the benefits of measures to help reconcile the demands and needs of family and professional life. Reconciliation, says the guide, has an important role to play in promoting gender equality; the well-being of children, parents, families, local communities and society; and improved economic performance. It "is a necessary condition for promoting gender equality in the labour market and thereby a better use of human resources."

► Chapter two, "What needs to be done? Policies and good practice", identifies the different levels at which action should be taken, emphasising that the national Government has a leading role to play. "It would be especially helpful," says the guide, "to define an overall, national policy and programme on reconciliation, to provide a context within which all other partners can develop their contributions."

► Chapter three, "How can it be done?", identifies the measures that can be taken to assist parents in the reconciliation of their work and family roles, see below.

► Chapter four, "Is it working? Monitoring, evaluation and review", stresses the need to monitor and evaluate policies and practices to see if they in fact "enable women and men to reconcile their occupation, family and upbringing responsibilities arising from the care of children." It lists the ways in which the measures taken can by monitored, evaluated and reviewed.

Below, we reproduce the Commission's suggestions on the measures that can be taken to aid work/family reconciliation, together with practical examples, in three areas covered by the Recommendation:
- ▶ leave arrangements for employed parents (article 4);
- ▶ the environment, structure and organisation of work and the workplace (article 5); and
- ▶ promoting and encouraging increased participation by men in the care of children (article 6).

Work and childcare: a guide to good practice
[...]

The role of the workplace

The policy framework
Providing a work environment which, to quote the Recommendation, takes into account "the needs of all working parents with responsibility for the care and upbringing of children" brings benefits to employers. They have been listed in Annex IV of this guide (Reconciliation: who benefits?). The present section describes some of the methods which can be used to achieve such an environment. But this is not a purely administrative issue. Like any other corporate system, a reconciliation policy depends for its success on strong support from senior management and an acceptance that employees have a life outside the workplace which places demands on them and which they have to relate to their working lives. A company and personnel philosophy which underlines the importance and legitimacy of family needs is necessary if working practices are to be supportive of those needs. This philosophy can be demonstrated by, for example:
- ▶ a wide and flexible range of employment options offered to all employees;
- ▶ a working culture which takes into account the rhythms of family and social life, and which therefore, for example, avoids as far as possible evening and weekend work;
- ▶ Codes of Practice or other clear statements of policy;
- ▶ full employment rights, career and training opportunities and status awarded to employees who take advantage of reconciliation practices on the same basis as those who do not need to use these practices;
- ▶ training for managers and supervisors in reconciliation and equal opportunities principles and practices;
- ▶ the provision of childcare services, directly or in partnership with other agencies, or through financial support to community services or to employees;
- ▶ a system of monitoring evaluation and review.

It is important that employees who take up any of the options listed below are not penalised for doing so. They should not be employed on less favourable terms and conditions. Nor should they be considered by their fellow-workers and/or managers as less committed to their work and hence excluded from training and promotion opportunities.

At present, and in spite of changes in the attitudes of some men, the main responsibility for childcare remains with mothers. Family-friendly practices, where they exist, tend therefore to be utilised by mothers. This can and does lead to increased job segregation and a vicious circle in which certain jobs are perceived as suitable for flexible working and hence become "women's jobs"; or else the jobs which women traditionally undertake are the only ones which are considered for flexible arrangements, hence excluding men from access to those arrangements; or flexible working arrangements are seen as designed for women and therefore somehow inappropriate for men.

Attitudes to the role of the father in the family are changing, and both men and women would like to be able to find a better balance between home and working life. It is likely that the companies who make it possible for employees to reconcile work and family will attract a highly-motivated, high-quality workforce.

Introducing a comprehensive reconciliation programme may well mean a significant change to the life of an organisation. It is important, therefore, that everyone involved in or affected by it, also believes in it. All employees, not just those who are parents, need to know why the policy is being introduced and what its effects will be.

The practices

Not all employees, not even all employees who are also working parents, form a homogeneous group. They will have different caring needs at different times of their and their children's lives, and at different stages in their own careers. Ideally, therefore, they need access to a range of options from which they and their employers can select the one which is most helpful to both parties.

This guide cannot give a detailed description of all the possible positive action measures which could be introduced into a workplace in order to answer the childcare needs of working parents. Moreover, many of these measures are part of providing good terms of employment for all employees, not just parents. The following list should be thought of as a menu from which to select, develop and implement those which are best suited to individual enterprises. However, it is important to make clear that all these practices have been successfully implemented in companies: that is, they are not a set of unreasonable demands by parents, but realistic, workable methods, of mutual benefit to employers and employees.

The most successful practices will be part of comprehensive reconciliation and/or equal opportunities policies.

1 Working time

Hours can be reduced by part-time working, by (temporarily) reduced working hours and by jobshare. Part-time working has historically been an option taken up by women and characterised by low pay and low status. Jobshare schemes are a more recent development and are less widely available, but generally carry better terms and conditions of employment than part-time work. It is not common yet for either option to be available at professional and managerial levels, although there is, in practice, little reason why this should be so.

> **Example**
>
> In 1990, Drs Hilary Matthews and Elizabeth Thompson were jointly appointed to the post of consultant anaesthetist at the Mater Infirmorum Hospital in Belfast, Northern Ireland. They had already been jobsharing a more junior post at another hospital, but their new appointment made them the most senior jobsharers in the United Kingdom National Health Service.

Hours can be staggered by shift work or flexitime. These options can include a very wide range of possibilities – term-time working, weekly shifts, three- or four-day weeks, weekly/monthly/annual balancing of hours.

Family needs are often as unpredictable as they are unavoidable; a sudden illness or accident involving a child or a carer does not necessarily require a parent to be present the whole day but requires that workers are able to react quickly in emergencies. Flexibility within the agreed work schedule is the ideal approach in these situations.

2 Flexiplace

Many jobs, and their number is increasing, can be carried out in the home. The most successful systems seem to be those in which work done at home is combined with regular contacts with the parent workplace or a network of other home workers, to avoid too great a sense of isolation. Flexiplace arrangements can be combined with flexible hours to create an extremely creative response to reconciling work and family responsibilities.

3 Career breaks/sabbaticals

These are usually for longer periods than parental leave, and may not be tied so specifically to the care of very young children. At the same time, however, as statutory leave arrangements become more flexible and longer, the difference between these two sets of measures is becoming less clear-cut.

Rather than prescribing a single model of these longer-term breaks, employers when consulting with workers may discover that, again, flexibility is the answer. Career breaks are being offered which range from two to seven or more years, depending on the use to which the employee wants to put the break. It is important to keep good contacts with the employee in her/his absence, through skills updating sessions, regular short periods of work, information on developments in the organisation, and careful re-entry training.

4   Leave arrangements for employed parents

The importance of a range of leave arrangements available to all workers has already been discussed. Basic entitlements may be improved in specific workplaces through collective or company agreements. Companies can also play an important role in ensuring that workers are fully informed of their statutory entitlements and are supported when they choose to use them.

5   The provision of company childcare or support services

Working parents report that their concentration and productivity at work is better if they are confident that their children are in safe and high-quality care. Some employers offer a variety of supportive measures, including:

- ▶   on-site childcare;
- ▶   referral systems to community childcare;
- ▶   company sponsorship of community childcare;
- ▶   childcare vouchers;
- ▶   children's holiday programmes;
- ▶   after-school programmes;
- ▶   company sponsorship of childcare training programmes;
- ▶   transport to and from childcare facilities; and
- ▶   lunch services for children of employees.

Examples**

Dragerwerk AG (Germany) This company actively encourages both men and women to take up flexible working patterns, the better to reconcile their work and family lives. They offer staff a "menu" of 50 different working arrangements, in order to allow them to choose the working hours which suit their domestic needs best.

Hopital St-Camille (France) This public organisation has arranged for the provision of various services to its staff and their families – such as ironing, cleaning, and the preparation of take-away hot meals.

It is important to note the earlier discussion in the section on providing care for children. Services supported by companies should meet the criteria and conditions outlined in that section. Employers' support for services may best be developed within the dual frameworks of a general national or regional policy on services, based on a clear model of service development. A local service should not depend in the long term on individual companies and the labour force needs of individual employers: this will lead to inequalities for children and parents. Wherever possible, workplace or employer-paid childcare services should supplement, and not replace, publicly supported provision, offering wider choice to parents in the area.

Sharing parental responsibilities

The Recommendation says that "Member states should promote and encourage, with due respect for the freedom of the individual, increased participation by men" (in the care and upbringing of children) [article 6]. The Recommendation recognises that increased participation of men in the care and upbringing of children is essential for reconciling employment and caring responsibilities in a way that promotes gender equality. It will lead to more equal sharing of parental and other family responsibilities between women and men. It will contribute to the mainstreaming of reconciliation. It will ensure that other reconciliation measures promote gender equality. Without increased participation by men in the care and upbringing of children, measures such as parental leave will be used mostly by women. This would confirm and reinforce employment inequalities as women, and not men, spend more time out of employment or working reduced hours.

Increased participation in the care and upbringing of children will require men to adopt new ways of working. At present, men typically work without a break throughout their adult lives, unless made unemployed. They work long hours in full-time jobs. This way of working presumes that men undertake few or no caring responsibilities; it is not compatible with equal sharing of family responsibilities. Unless this changes, women will continue to carry the greater share of family responsibilities – while having to emulate men's way of working if they wish to compete successfully in employment. For those women who cannot, or do not wish to, emulate men's way of working, the alternative will be to accept ways of working which do recognise family responsibilities (for example, jobsharing, part-time work), but which at present make it difficult or impossible to compete in the labour market with men.

Genuine equality between men and women requires not only more equal sharing in the home, but also that both men and women adopt new ways of working that recognise family responsibilities. The organisation of home life and work life are inextricably connected.

A reconciliation policy – adopted at government, social partner or individual workplace level – should "make an explicit commitment to the importance of achieving a more equal sharing of family responsibilities between men and women" [Parliament opinion].

All other measures taken to promote reconciliation – provision of services, leave arrangements, workplace developments and any others should be "compatible with this objective" [ibid.]. This is more likely to be achieved by:

▶ Developing closer relations between services and parents which in turn requires a commitment and action to involve fathers as well as mothers in services and to increase the number of men working with children in services††.

▶ Structuring leave arrangements in such a way that they positively encourage fathers to take leave, for example through: the provision of paternity leave and of parental leave and leave for family reasons that is equally available to fathers and mothers; limited non-transferability; and where possible some compensation for lost earnings.

► Making workplace measures equally available to men and women and structuring them in such a way that they positively encourage fathers as well as mothers to take advantage of them.

Clear political commitment and ensuring all reconciliation measures are compatible are both important. A broad and coherent strategy for promoting change might embrace the following objectives:

► Increasing public awareness and modifying public expectations about men's responsibility for children;
► Enabling men to appreciate the benefits to them, and others, of a greater participation in the care of their children and the development of closer relationships;
► Addressing the concerns of parents, childcare workers and the general public about men participating more in the care of children; and
► Identifying and tackling obstacles and constraints – at individual, family, workplace and societal levels – that hinder and discourage increased participation by men, and developing effective ways of enabling individuals and organisations to change.

The strategy emphasises the need to encourage and support change, and to remove constraints, thereby increasing the freedom of the individual. It does not coerce or pressurise men and women to adopt attitudes and behaviour that are not acceptable to them. It recognises that achieving change will be a complex and slow process, and that there are important resistances which need to be treated with sensitivity***.

This involves exploring and evaluating the contribution of a variety of measures. As well as an explicit policy commitment and other, compatible, reconciliation measures, more specific measures have a role to play and may include:

► work in schools, concerning parenthood, gender and childcare;
► work with prospective and actual parents (including programmes exclusively for fathers) in various settings (for example, the workplace, hospitals, health centres, nurseries and services for children);
► workplace programmes, involving employers and employees, to change the culture of work organisations, and to find effective ways of putting policies into practice and to deal with barriers to change;
► training for the social partners at national and regional level;
► media programmes and other methods of raising public awareness and modifying expectations.

Finally, an effective strategy needs to be based on careful monitoring and research into the most effective ways of bringing about change. The involvement of men and women in services, leave arrangements and workplace measures needs to be monitored and studied. Research needs to be undertaken in a variety of settings to understand better how and why change occurs and how the process of change can be best supported.

Example

The regional government of Emilia-Romagna in Italy began its "Fatherhood Project" in 1992. The project has three parts.

First, research into fatherhood. The researchers from the Universities of Bologna and Parma interviewed individual fathers and groups of fathers and mothers. They asked them about fathers' role, identity and life experiences, the effect of the birth of their children, their involvement in the care of their children and in housework, their relationships with their partners and how they reconciled work and family life.

Secondly, mothers and fathers of children attending childcare services in Emilia-Romagna have taken part in discussion groups which covered old and new models of maternity and paternity, how families are organised, how partners work together and gender identity.

Thirdly, several nurseries in Emilia-Romagna and a centre in Corby in the United Kingdom have come together to explore ways of increasing the part fathers play in childcare services and how centres can help fathers and mothers to think about gender roles and relationships. One objective of this initiative has been to identify strategies which could be applied throughout Europe, taking very different social, economic and cultural settings into account.

* "Work and childcare: implementing the Council recommendation on childcare – a guide to good practice". Social Europe – Supplement 5/96. Available from The Stationery
Office, tel: 0171 873 9090, price on request.

† A longer discussion on leave arrangements, with figures for 16 countries, is contained in EC Network on Childcare and Other Measures to Reconcile Employment and Family. Responsibilities for Men and Women (1994), "Leave arrangements for workers with children", Brussels: Commission of the European Communities.

** These examples both come from companies which won their categories of the European Social Innovation Prize, awarded at Stockholm in May 1995. Further details of prizewinners are available from Unit V/E/1 of the European Commission, 200 Rue de la Loi, B-1049 Brussels.

†† Two publications by the EC Childcare Network cover this area: "Fathers, nurseries and childcare" and "Men as workers in childcare services" – both available from the Commission (DGV/D/5).

*** See report of "Ravenna seminar on men as carers", produced by EC Childcare Network and available from the Commission (V/D/5).

Appendix 3

Useful statistics

1   Part-time workers

a   Male and female part-time workers in the labour market and hours worked

Part-time employees by sex, average total usual hours of work, Spring, 1984, 1990, 1997 are as follows:

Men	1984	1990	1997
P/t male employees as a percentage of all male employees	2.6	3.8	7.5
Average usual weekly hours of work	16.5	15.4	16.7

Women			
P/t female employees as a percentage of all female employees	42.3	41.1	42.9
Average usual weekly hours of work	18.3	18.0	18.4

Note: the average usual weekly hours of work include paid and unpaid overtime but excludes meal breaks.[1]

b Male and female part-time workers broken down by marital status and industry: Autumn 1997, GB, thousands

	Male		Female	
	Married /cohab.	Other	Married /cohab.	Other
All industries	297	545	3,337	1,187
Agriculture & fishing	*	*	18	*
Energy & Water	*	*	10	*
Manufacturing	32	32	215	44
Construction	10	*	48	*
Distribution, hotels & restaurants	60	333	885	615
Transport & communication	34	23	93	24
Banking, finance & insurance etc	35	35	386	79
Public admin, education & health	92	59	1,492	309
Other services	31	51	187	100

Note: includes those who did not specify their industry and those whose work-place is outside the UK.
* = sample size too small to provide a reliable estimate.[2]

2 Weekly hours of work by age of youngest dependent child for full-time and part-time employees by sex: Autumn 1997

| | **Male employees with:** | | | | | |
| | No dependent children | | Youngest child 0-4 | | Youngest child 5+ | |
	F/T	P/T	F/T	P/T	F/T	P/T
% working f/p-t	90.7	9.3	96.9	3.1	97.4	2.6
Average total usual hours	45.2	17.0	46.8	19.6	47.0	20.9
Average basic usual hours	40.7	15.8	41.3	18.4	41.6	19.9
Average total usual overtime	4.6	1.2	5.4	1.2	5.4	1.0

| | **Female employees with:** | | | | | |
| | No dependent children | | Youngest child 0-4 | | Youngest child 5+ | |
	F/T	P/T	F/T	P/T	F/T	P/T
% working f/p-t	68.8	31.2	36.0	63.9	41.4	58.6
Average total usual hours	41.2	18.5	39.9	18.2	40.4	19.4
Average basic usual hours	38.0	17.3	37.2	17.1	36.8	17.9
Average total usual overtime	3.1	1.2	2.7	1.2	3.6	1.5

Note: average total usual hours includes paid and unpaid overtime. Paid and unpaid overtime derived by subtracting basic hours from total hours.[3]

3   Job-shares

	All persons	Males	Females
Employees in j/s (thous)	177	18	158
(%)	100	10	89
Employees in j/s as % of all employees	0.8	0.2	1.54

4   Male and female employees who only work during school terms: Autumn 1997

	All persons	Males	Females
Employed in education	774	139	634
Other employees	177	16	159[5]

Footnotes

1 Answer to PQ 22.4.98: Source Labour force Survey (LFS), ONS

2 Answer to PQ 22.4.98: Source LFS.

3 Answer to PQ 22.4.98: Source LFS

4 Answer to PQ 22.4.98: Source LFS

5 Answer to PQ 11.4.98: Source LFS

Appendix 4

Useful addresses

Bar Pro Bono Unit
7 Gray's Inn Square
London
WC1R 5AZ
0171 831 9711
F: 0171 831 9733.

Equal Opportunities Commission
Overseas House
Quay Street
Manchester M3 3HN
0161 833-9244.

**Federation of Independent
Advice Centres**
4 Deans Court
St Paul's Churchyard
London EC4V 5AA
0171 489 1800

Law Centres Federation
London Office:
Duchess House
18-19 Warren Street
London W1P 5DB
0171 387- 8570

Sheffield Office
3rd Floor
Arundel Court
177 Arundel Street
Sheffield S1 2NU
01142 787088.

Mary Ward Legal Centre
26-27 Boswell Street
London WC1N 3JZ
0171 831 7079

Maternity Alliance
45 Beech Street
London EC2P 2LX
Advice line: 0171 588-8582
Office: 0171 588-8583
*or send an s.a.e. for
a publications list*

New Ways to Work
309 Upper Street
London N1 2TY
0171 226 4026

Rights of Women
52-54 Featherstone Street
London EC1V 8RT
0171 251-6575

Appendix 5

Bibliography

Statistical and background formation

Family-friendly working arrangements in Britain 1996 DfEE Research Report RR16 PSI 1997.

The Family Friendly Employer: Examples from Europe Daycare Trust 1992

Women and Organisations Change Angela Coyle EOC 1995

Job-Sharing: Putting Policy into Practice New Ways to Work 1987

The Best of Both Worlds: the benefits of a flexible approach to working arrangements: A guide for employers Employment Department

Flexibility in Practice: Women's Employment and Pay in Retail and Finance by Fiona Neathey and Jennifer Hurstfield Industrial Relations Service 1995

Effective Ways of Recruiting and Retaining Women IRS 1990

Family Friendly Working Institute of Manpower Studies (IMS) 1992

About Time: The Revolution in Work and Family Life Patricia Hewitt IPPR 1993

Changing Times: A Guide to Flexible Work Patterns for Human Resource Managers New Ways to Work 1993

Job Sharing: Putting Policy into Practice New Ways to Work 1987

Change at the Top: Working flexibly at senior and managerial levels in organisations New Ways to Work 1994

Flexibility Abused: evidence on employment conditions in the labour market CAB 1997

Part-time Work Directive: What it means for UK employees: guidelines and commentary TUC 1997

Workplace Culture – Long Hours High Stress? Report of a Seminar arranged by the Women's National Commission 1995

Maternity Alliance publications

Leaflets for employees (send an s.a.e.):

Child-friendly working hours: your legal rights	£1.50
Pregnant at work	£1.50
Returning to work	£2.00
Having it all: a woman's guide to combining breastfeeding and work	£2.00
or write for a full publications list	

For employers:

Pregnancy and Maternity: The law and practice	£17.00
Breastfeeding and work	£6.00

Guides to the law published by Legal Action Group

Maternity Rights by Camilla Palmer (with Maternity Alliance) 1996

Discrimination at Work by Camilla Palmer, Gay Moon and Susan Cox (3rd ed) 1997

Employment Law: An Advisers' Handbook by Kibling and Lewis (3rd ed) 1996

Employment Tribunal Procedure by McMullen QC and Eady 1996

EOC publications

A Step by Step Guide to Taking a Case to an Industrial Tribunal in England and Wales

Compensation in Sex Discrimination Cases post-Marshall

Appendix 6

Glossary and abbreviations

Actual week of childbirth (AWC)
This is the week when the baby is born. The 29 weeks maternity absence starts from the beginning of the **actual** week of childbirth. A week usually starts on a Sunday.

11th week before the EWC
The 11th week is the earliest date on which general maternity leave can start (unless the baby is born before then). A week runs from Sunday to Saturday.

ACAS (Advisory, Conciliation, Arbitration Service)
ACAS officers are sent the IT1 and IT3 by the tribunal. They will contact each party to try and encourage settlement.

Applicant
The applicant is the person bringing a complaint of discrimination.

Complainant
The same as the applicant, though the person asking questions in the questionnaire is referred to as the complainant.

Directions hearing
This is a hearing when the tribunal will make orders about how the case is to be run (eg, whether there should be discovery, further and better particulars, how long the hearing will take).

Expected week of childbirth (EWC)
This is the week the baby is due. It begins at midnight on the Saturday, so the first day is Sunday.

Further and Better Particulars
This can be requested by letter (or formal pleading document) and is a way of getting further details from the other side about their case as set out in the Notice of Application (IT1 or Notice of Appearance (IT3).

Maternity certificate (MATB1)

This is the certificate given to the woman by her doctor or midwife. It will show the date when the baby is due.

Notice of Application (IT1)

This is the form on which the application to the tribunal is made.

Notice of Appearance (IT3)

This is the employer's response to the IT1.

Party

The parties are the applicant and the respondent(s).

Questionnaire

This enables the applicant to ask questions about the way she has been treated and why.

Respondent

This is the person(s) against whom the proceedings are being taken. The respondent will be the applicant's employer, but may also be an employment agency, a trade union, a partner, a training body.

Written questions and answers

Either party can ask the other written questions where this will help clarify issues. If the party refuses to answer, the tribunal can make an order.

Abbreviations

ACAS	Advisory Conciliation and Arbitration Service
Art 119	EC Treaty article 119
CA	Court of Appeal
DCLD	Discrimination Case Law Digest
DfEE	Department of Education and Employment
DTI	Department of Trade and Industry
EAT	Employment Appeal Tribunal
EC	European Community
ECJ	European Court of Justice
EOC	Equal Opportunities Commission
EOR	Equal Opportunities Review
EPD	Equal Pay Directive
ERA	Employment Rights Act 1996
EqPA	Equal Pay Act 1970
ETD	Equal Treatment Directive
EWC	Expected week of childbirth
FRU	Free Representation Unit
HL	House of Lords
IRLR	Industrial Relations Law Reports
IT	Industrial Tribunal
IT1	Notice of Application
IT3	Notice of Appearance
JSA	Job seeker's allowance
LEL	Lower Earnings Limit
LFS	Labour Force Survey
NACAB	National Association of Citizen's Advice Bureaux
NICA	Northern Ireland Court of Appeal
SDA	Sex Discrimination Act 1975
SMP	Statutory maternity pay
SSP	Statutory s`ick pay
ROW	Rights of Women

Appendix 7

Precedents: standard forms and example letters

The following are examples of documents which are intended to give some idea of what might be covered in different situations. Obviously, it is important that the documents are adapted to suit the circumstances of each case.

1 Letter requesting child-friendly hours

Further to our recent discussion, I am writing to say that I was very upset that you will not allow me to job-share or work shorter hours and would ask that you review your decision.

As you know, I cannot work full-time [continue to work such long hours] [work after 5.30pm] because of [my childcare arrangements]. I have suggested various options to you, [including working from home one day a week or job-sharing or working through lunch to enable me to leave earlier] but you have rejected these. I am prepared to be flexible and consider other arrangements which you may consider more suitable.

I believe your refusal to be discriminatory and would draw your attention to the enclosed leaflet by Maternity Alliance.

If you do not agree to allow me to change my hours I feel I have no choice but to resign.

Note
Never threaten to resign until you have made a decision that you will do so if refused the requested hours.

2 Letter of resignation

I am writing to confirm that I cannot continue to work for the company and am giving you one month's notice.

As you know, the reason I am leaving is because you have refused to allow me to reduce my hours [or job-share] [work from home for one day a week] and I cannot continue working full-time. I believe this is sex discrimination and unfair constructive dismissal.

3 Draft Letter Before Action to Employer after a refusal to allow job-share/part-time work in the same job

We are acting for Ms S. who has been employed as a personal assistant to the Managing Director since March 1990.

In June 1997, our client informed you that she was pregnant, that she would be taking maternity leave from November 1997 and wanted to return to the same job.

In March 1998, our client confirmed, in response to your request, that she would be returning to work. At the same time she asked if she could return either part-time or on a job-share basis. You said that you would consider this.

On 2 April 1998 you wrote to our client offering her a part-time position as secretary to the Department, saying that this was an equivalent position. You informed our client that her maternity locum had been appointed permanently as personal assistant to the Managing Director.

Refusal to allow our client to return to the job in which she was employed prior to her maternity absence is a deemed dismissal.

It is clear that the reason our client was not allowed to return was because of her pregnancy, childbirth and/or maternity leave absence or alternatively because she had asked to work part-time. In either case, the dismissal is automatically unfair and discriminatory.

Further and in the alternative, the relationship of trust and confidence has clearly broken down as a result of the fundamental breach of our client's contract, thus entitling our client to claim constructive dismissal and sex discrimination.

Further, the refusal to allow our client to work part-time in the job in which she was employed prior to going on maternity leave is indirectly discriminatory on the grounds of sex. As you are aware, our client is unable to work full-time because she has been unable to find suitable and affordable childcare.

Our client is extremely unhappy and distressed about the way she has been treated. If we do not hear from you, within seven days, with an offer of substantial compensation for the loss she has suffered, including injury to feelings, we will be submitting a questionnaire under the Sex Discrimination Act and lodging a complaint for unfair dismissal and sex discrimination.

4 SDA Questionnaire

Paragraph 2

1   The complainant [I, (if the woman is unrepresented)] started working for the respondents in April 1990. The respondents are a large organisation, employing approximately 80 secretarial and administrative staff.

2   The complainant went on maternity leave in May 1997. She then asked if she could reduce her hours on her return. She was told that the situation would be reviewed.

3   The complainant returned to work in January 1998 and asked again to work part-time or job-share. She was told that this was not possible.
4   The complainant could not continue working full-time and felt she had no alternative but to resign, which she did by letter dated 1st September 1998.
5   The complainant has been discriminated against on the grounds of sex by being required to work full-time.

Alternatively, if the IT1 has been lodged, question 2 can be answered by referring to the IT1 – ie, 'see IT1 attached'.

Paragraph 6

1   Please provide a copy of your equal opportunities policy and any policy on job sharing.
2   Please state what criteria are used when deciding to allow an employee to work part-time, reduced hours or to job-share and provide any relevant documents.
3   Please state who is responsible for making a decision about whether an employee can work part-time or job-share.
4   Please provide a breakdown of employees who have been employed as secretarial or administrative staff over the last three years stating in each case:
     i   their sex and marital status;
     ii   whether they work full-time or part-time and if part-time whether reduced hours or job-share;
     iii   their grade, job title and location.
5   Please state how many employees have in the past three years made a request to work reduced hours or job-share or to work part-time and whether in each case their request was allowed or refused. In each case please state:
a   job title, grade, location,
b   whether male or female,
     c   nature of request and reasons for making it,
     d   date and reason for refusal,
     e   whether the employee left the Company as a result of the refusal and, if so, for what reason.
     Please provide relevant documents.
6   Please give details of the proportion of women over the last three years who returned after maternity leave, stating in each case whether they returned:
     a   to full-time employment;
     b   to part-time employment;
7   Do you agree that John S. initially agreed that the complainant could return to work on a part-time basis after the complainant said that had problems finding suitable childcare.
8   Please state in relation to the complainant:
     a   what steps were taken to investigate whether the complainant could job-share or work part-time;

  b whose decision it was to refuse the option;

  c who was consulted, on what dates, and what were their views.

  Please provide any relevant documents, including memos, letters, minutes etc.

9 Please give full details of the complainant's job description and duties as under-taken in practice.

10 Please state precisely why the complainant's post could not be done part-time, on reduced hours or on a job-share basis, stating in relation to each:

  a why the type of queries and nature of workload required a level of continuity throughout the week and why continuity was 'mandatory';

  b what arrangements are made during holiday, sickness and maternity absence and, if not satisfactory, why not.

11 Please provide a list of all administrative, clerical and secretarial vacancies between June 1997 and June 1998 and state whether:

  a the vacancy was full-time or part-time or available on a job-share basis;

  b it was filled by a full-time or part-time employee or on a job-share basis.

12 Please provide a copy of the complainant's personnel file.

5 IT1: Notice of Application: Details of complaint (Section 11)

1 The Applicant was employed by the Respondents as a typist. She commenced work on 1 December 1990.

2 The Applicant was promoted on several occasions and in or about January 1995 became an administrator.

3 At appraisals during 1995 the Applicant's work was commended.

4 On or about 15 November 1997 the Applicant gave the Respondents her Maternity Certificate (MAT B1) which showed that the expected week of childbirth was the week beginning 11 February 1998.

8 On 22 November 1997 the Applicant gave written notice that she would start her maternity leave on 8 January 1998. She stated that she intended to return to work after the birth of her baby.

9 The Applicant commenced her maternity leave on 8 January 1998 and her baby was born on 2 February 1998.

10 The Applicant was entitled to return to work in the job in which she was employed before she went on maternity leave.

11 On 1 September 1998 the Applicant wrote to the Respondents requesting that she return to work on a part-time or job-share basis.

12 On 6 September 1998 the Respondents wrote to the Applicant stating that there was no possibility of a part-time position or job-share arrangement.

13 The Applicant was not able to return to work full-time because she was unable to make satisfactory childcare arrangements. The Applicant felt she had no alternative but to resign, which she did by letter sent on 23 September 1998. By virtue of the Respondents' conduct towards her she was entitled to terminate her contract.

In the circumstances, the Applicant considers that she has been constructively unfairly dismissed and has suffered discrimination.

14   The requirement to work full-time is indirectly discriminatory on the grounds of sex.

15   Further and in the alternative, the Respondents failed to follow their own job-sharing policy.

16   The Applicant claims:

    a   a declaration that she has suffered sex discrimination;

    c   a recommendation that she be considered for a job on a job-share or part-time basis;

    d   compensation for unfair constructive dismissal and sex discrimination, including injury to feelings.

6   IT3: Notice of Appearance by Respondents

1   The Applicant's request to work part-time was refused because the nature of the job requires a full-time employee and because she was an unreliable employee with a poor attendance record.

2   The refusal of the Applicant's request was justified.

3   It is denied that the Applicant was dismissed. She resigned.

4   It is denied that the Respondents discriminated against the Applicant.

7   Request for Further and Better Particulars of the IT3

Paragraph 1

Of 'The Applicant's request to work part-time was refused because the nature of the job requires a full-time employee and because she was an unreliable employee with a poor attendance record', please provide details of the following:

a   why the nature of the job requires a full-time employee, giving all facts and matters relied on, including:

    i   who made the decision that the nature of the job requires a full-time employee and when;

    ii   all factors taken into account when reaching this decision.

b   details of all facts and matters relied on to show that the Applicant was an unreliable employee, including:

    i   dates and times when it is alleged she was unreliable;

    ii   whether the alleged unreliability was raised with the Applicant, on what dates, by whom and what was said;

    iii   whether it is alleged that the Applicant was more unreliable than other employees and if so giving details of those other employees.

c   details of all facts and matters relied on to show that the Applicant had a poor attendance record, including:

    i   dates and times when it is alleged the applicant's attendance was poor;

    ii   whether the alleged poor attendance was raised with the Applicant, on what dates, by whom and what was said;

    iii   whether it is alleged that the Applicant had a worse attendance record than other employees and if so, giving details of those other employees.

The Respondent is requested to reply within 14 days and to provide all documents relevant to the above matters, including but not limited to letters, memoranda, notes, information held on the computer, and records.

8   Applicant's witness statement

In the Ashford Employment Tribunal

Between	Jane Smith	Applicant
and	Fixit limited	Respondents

Witness statement of applicant

1   I, Jane S., of .... will say as follows:

2   I have worked for the respondents as a secretary and administrator to a Director since June 1990.

3   In July 1997 I told the director, for whom I work, John S. that I was pregnant, that I planned to take maternity leave and then return to work.

4   I gave written notice that I was pregnant on..................... and that I intended to start my maternity leave on..................... I confirmed in the letter that I intended to return to work.

5   In about November 1997 I raised with John S. the possibility of returning to work on a job-share basis. I told him that another secretary in the same department, Helen, also wants to job-share and I thought we could job-share my job. John S. said he would consider the possibility, raise it with the Management Team and get back to me. At the time he seemed to be reluctant and asked how it would work in practice.

6   I went on maternity leave on..................... At this time no-one had said any more about my request to work part-time.

7   When the respondents wrote to me asking me whether I intended to return to work, I replied saying that I did intend to return and still wanted to work part-time or job-share. I explained, in the letter, that I had found a very good childminder who lived in the same street, that she could only work three days a week but was willing to be flexible about the hours, so that I could stay late occasionally.

8   I gave 21 days notice of my return to work on 21 July 1998.

9   On 25 July I was asked to go into the office for a meeting with my boss, John S. and a representative from personnel. I was then told that I could work part-time as a floating secretary for the whole department, but could not return to my old job working for the Director. I was stunned by this and said that I wanted my old job back and did not see why I could not do that part-time. I was told that I could

choose between my old job full-time or the alternative job part-time. I was assured that the new job had potential and was equivalent.

10 In the circumstances I felt I had no alternative but to try out the new job as floating secretary. I made it clear to the respondents that I was only doing this under protest.

11 After a month of doing the new job, it was clear that it was not suitable. Apart from the fact that I was mainly an audio typist, when previously I had been a personal assistant, I was also obliged to take instructions from the person who took over my job. I wrote to personnel on..................... pointing this out and asking to be reinstated in my old job. I asked for a meeting with personnel to discuss this.

12 At a meeting with..................... from personnel, I was told that my maternity locum had been appointed permanently to my old job and it was no longer available. The only job was the floating secretary. I said I was very unhappy about this and felt that I had no alternative but to resign and claim unfair dismissal and discrimination.

13 On..................... I wrote to the respondents saying that I felt I had been denied my job back, that they had discriminated against me and I felt I could no longer continue working for the company.

14 I believe that it would have been possible to do my old job as a job-share. Both Helen R and I had worked for the department for many years so were familiar with all the systems and knew the clients. For example, all the meetings are diarised on the computer and I had agreed with Helen that we would have an overlap of an hour on a Wednesday and would be available by telephone on the days we were not working if any problems arose. We made it clear to the respondents that we were willing to be flexible.

15 I had explained to the respondents that I could not work full-time because:
   ▶   I had not been able to find a suitable childminder who would work full-time;
   ▶   I have a long way to travel and my partner worked long hours and was often not back until 8pm;
   ▶   I felt the long hours would be too stressful and I knew how tired I felt previously when working long hours;
   ▶   I have another child, aged 5, who has just started school and need to go and see the teachers periodically.

16 I believe I could easily have worked as a secretary and administrator for John S. on a job-share basis and the refusal to allow me to do this was unjustified. I believe this was discriminatory.

Question 1. Has the Respondent applied a requirement or condition to the applicant?

It is a requirement or condition of continued employment by the Respondents that the Applicant work full-time.

Requirement/condition should be widely interpreted. They are words 'fully capable (for example) of including an obligation of full-time work'; see *Holmes v Home Office* [1984] IRLR 299 at p301.

In *United Distillers v Gordon* (unreported EAT/12/97), the EAT adopted the reasoning of Browne-Wilkinson J in *Clarke v Eley (IMI) Kynock Ltd* [1982] IRLR 482 which was quoted with approval by Hutton LCJ in *Briggs v North Eastern Education and Library Board* [1990] IRLR 181, 'The purpose of the legislature in introducing the concept of indirect discrimination into the 1975 Act... was to seek to eliminate those practices which had a disproportionate impact on women... and were not justifiable for other reasons... If the elimination of such practices is the policy lying behind the Act, although such policy cannot be used to give the words any wider meaning than they naturally bear it is in our view a powerful argument against giving the words a narrower meaning thereby excluding cases which fall within the mischief which the Act was meant to deal with'.

[In *Gordon*, the EAT said: 'We consider that Clymo is isolated, and correctly so'.]

Question 2: Does the requirement or condition disproportionately disadvantage women?

The test is whether a considerably smaller proportion of women than men can comply with the requirement 'to work full-time'.

a   Labour market statistics show that:

83% of part-time employees are women. About 47% of female employees work part-time, compared to about 5% of male employees (Table 2 of the LFS Quarterly Bulletin (March 1998)

▶ four out of five women working part-time (compared with two in five men) do not want a full-time job (Office for National Statistics, Labour Market Trends, vol. 105, no. 1, Jan. 1997).

▶ 57.1% of female employees can work full-time compared to 92.5% of men (Labour Force Survey, see p00);

In *London Underground v Edwards No 2* [998] IRLR 364, the CA held that:

a   the purpose of the SDA is to set out a 'threshold for intervention' where there exists a substantial and not merely marginal discriminatory effect;

b   the tribunal must be confident that the disparate impact is inherent in the application of the requirement or condition and not simply the product of unreliable statistics or fortuitous circumstance;

c   the 'pool' was those employees to whom the requirement (new rostering arrangements in *Edwards*) applied; however, the tribunal were entitled to take note of the high number of single mothers having care of children compared to the number of single fathers;

d   tribunal members do not sit in 'blinkers' and are entitled to take account of their knowledge and expertise;

e   the tribunal was right to take account of the large discrepancy in numbers of male and female staff in the pool (there were over 2,000 men and 23 women). The small number of female train drivers showed that it was either difficult or unattractive for women to work as train drivers; thus the difference between 95.2% of women who 'could comply' and 100% of men was 'considerably smaller'; this figure should be regarded as a minimum rather than a maximum.

In *Briggs*, the NICA said that a tribunal can take into account its own knowledge and experience when deciding whether a requirement has a disproportionate impact and elaborate statistical evidence was not always necessary.

b   Impact of requirement amongst similar employees in workforce

The relevant pool is the number of men and women to whom the employer applies or would apply the requirement, ie administrative assistants.

Of a total of 60 female employees, 45 work full-time and 15 part-time. Thus 75% can comply with the requirement to work full-time.

Of a total of 100 male employees, 95 work full-time and 5 part-time. Thus 95% can comply with the requirement to work full-time.

A considerably smaller proportion of women than men (20% difference) can comply with the requirement to work full-time.

Take from table on p37.

Taking into account:

a   the tribunal's own knowledge and experience that women bear primary responsibility for children,

b   the LFS figures which show that the vast majority of part-time workers are women,

c   the fact that women work part-time by choice, because of childcare, and

d   in this particular case in the relevant pool a considerably smaller proportion of women than men – ie 20% – can comply with the requirement,

the Applicant has proved disproportionate impact.

Question 3: Is the requirement to the applicant's detriment because she cannot comply with it?

The test is as set out in *Price v Civil Service Commission* [1977] IRLR 291, when the EAT said that a woman:

'is not obliged to marry, or to have children, or to mind children; she may find somebody to look after them and as a last resort she may put them into care. However, to say that for those reasons she can comply with a requirement to work full-time would be 'wholly out of sympathy with the spirit and intent of the Act. It is relevant in determining whether women can comply with the condition to take into account the current usual behaviour of women in this respect as observed in practice, putting aside behaviour and responses which are unusual'.

In *United Distillers v Gordon* unreported EAT/12/97 23.5.97 the EAT said that:
'although nursery facilities can be made available, we do not consider that precludes the view that a mother with child-caring responsibilities meets the non-compliance test. We recognise that each case would have to be looked at carefully to look at the practical implications of compliance, but there can be little doubt that a mother with a very young baby is at least capable of meeting the test'.

The Applicant cannot comply with the requirement to work full-time for the following reasons...

The Applicant suffered a detriment because... [she was forced to resign because she could not work full-time].

Question 4: Has the employer justified the requirement to work full-time?

The burden of proof is on the Respondents to show justification.

The discriminatory effect of the requirement must be balanced against the good and sound reason why the business needed such a requirement (*Hampson v Department of Education and Science* [1989] IRLR 69

In *United Distillers v Gordon* the EAT, following *Hampson*, held that:
'the justification advanced by the employer had to be objectively established. It was not sufficient that the employer believed his reasons behind the decision to be justified'.

'What has to be justified, in terms of the legislation, is the requirement or condition imposed which is said to be discriminatory, judged objectively, and, accordingly, it is wholly inappropriate, in our opinion, to decide the matter by determining the subjective approach in fact of the employer. It is not sufficient in law that the employer be satisfied in his own mind that the decision is justifiable on reasons good to him... it is an objective external judgment of those elements that is required to determine the issue in favour of the employer'.
The employer has failed to show the requirement (to work full-time) was justified.

Advisory Conciliation and Arbitration Service (ACAS)

Tribunal case number

....

Agreement in respect of an application made to the tribunal

Applicant   **Respondent**

Name   ....

Address   ....

            ....

            ....

Settlement reached as a result of a conciliation action.

We the undersigned have agreed that:

1   The Respondent will pay the Applicant the sum of £15,000 in respect of all out-
        standing claims before the tribunal, such payment to be made within 14 days of
        the date of this agreement.

2   The Respondent will provide the Applicant with a reference in the attached form
        or in no worse terms, to anyone seeking a reference in respect of the Applicant's
        employment with the Respondent.

and/or

The Respondent will allow the Applicant to work 18 hours per week with effect from...

[Note, if the agreement is done through a relevant independent adviser, not ACAS, there will be an extra clause stating:

The Applicant confirms that, before signing the agreement, she received independent legal advice from... [name of independent legal adviser], of ... as to the terms and effect of this agreement and, in particular, its effect on her ability to pursue her rights before an employment tribunal.

The regulations relating to compromise agreements under the ERA and SDA are satisfied under this agreement.

Signed by the Applicant or her representative ....

Dated ....

Signed by the Respondent ....

Dated ....

Table of cases

Index

P